WHAT PEOPLE ARE

You Can Take It with You!

Does your quality of life in heaven depend on how you've readied yourself on earth? When Jesus said to prepare treasures for yourself in heaven, do those treasures vary according to how you prepared? Doug Schmidt courageously addresses the questions that many of us have about life after death, but few have answered clearly.

MARSHALL SHELLEY
EDITOR, *LEADERSHIP*
VICE PRESIDENT, CHRISTIANITY TODAY INTERNATIONAL

If you think heaven is a "someday" thing, just read You Can Take It with You! *Doug Schmidt shows you how the hereafter is here today.*

STEVE GRISSOM
PRESIDENT, CHURCH INITIATIVE

In this ground-breaking book, Doug reminds us that no act of kindness done in the name of Jesus goes unrewarded. After every chapter, you'll be refreshed and invigorated to keep giving your best to the Master.

TIM WILSON
PASTOR, INDIAN HILLS CHRISTIAN FELLOWSHIP, INDIAN HILLS, COLORADO

Doug Schmidt delivers a wonderfully fresh, biblically informed treatment on the importance of everyday life and its impact on eternity in You Can Take It with You! *Dare to ask yourself the question "How much does God trust me?"*

STEVE WAMBERG
AUTHOR, *PINOCCHIO NATION: EMBRACING TRUTH IN A CULTURE OF LIES*

THE MOST IMPORTANT QUESTION IS NOT

"DO YOU TRUST GOD?"

BUT RATHER

"HOW MUCH DOES HE TRUST YOU?"

WELL DONE, MY GOOD SERVANT! ... BECAUSE YOU HAVE BEEN TRUSTWORTHY IN A VERY SMALL MATTER, TAKE CHARGE OF TEN CITIES.

LUKE 19:17

You Can Take It With You!

Doug Schmidt

Victor®
The Bible Teacher's Teacher

COOK COMMUNICATIONS MINISTRIES
Colorado Springs, Colorado • Paris, Ontario
KINGSWAY COMMUNICATIONS LTD
Eastbourne, England

Victor® is an imprint of
Cook Communications Ministries Colorado Springs, Colorado 80918
Cook Communications, Paris, Ontario
Kingsway Communications, Eastbourne, England

YOU CAN TAKE IT WITH YOU!
© 2006 by Doug Schmidt

All rights reserved. No part of this book may be reproduced without written permission, except for brief quotations in books and critical reviews. For information, write Cook Communications Ministries, 4050 Lee Vance View, Colorado Springs, Colorado 80918.

Cover Design: Identity Design
Cover Photo: iStockPhoto

The Web addresses (URLs) recommended throughout this book are solely offered as a resource to the reader. The citation of these Web sites does not in any way imply an endorsement on the part of the author or the publisher, nor does the author or publisher vouch for their content for the life of this book.

First printing, 2006
Printed in the United States of America

1 2 3 4 5 6 7 8 9 10 Printing / Year 10 09 08 07 06

All Scripture quotations, unless otherwise noted, are taken from the *Holy Bible, New International Version*®. *NIV*®. Copyright © 1973, 1978, 1984 by International Bible Society. Used by permission of Zondervan. All rights reserved. Scripture quotations marked NASB are taken from the *New American Standard Bible,* © Copyright 1960, 1995 by The Lockman Foundation. Used by permission; and KJV are taken from the King James Version of the Bible. (Public Domain.) All italics in Scripture have been added by the author for emphasis.

ISBN-13: 978-0-7814-4229-9
ISBN-10: 0-7814-4229-X

LCCN: 2006925620

To Kate, Nate, and Christianna

Contents

Preface:
    Beginning at the End 9
1. The Final Dominion:
    Humans Ruling Where Angels Fear to Tread 15
2. Protestant Purgatory:
    The Bema Seat Judgment........................... 29
3. Peter's Vocational Test for Kingdom Placement:
    Characteristics of the Person God Trusts 45
4. Grace:
    Jesus' Personal Relationship with the Unsaved 59
5. Faith:
    Belief and Repentance—a Two-Sided Coin.............. 81
6. Goodness:
    Engaging a Hostile Culture without
    Losing Your Identity 92
7. Knowledge:
    A Genuine Desire to Understand 109
8. Self-Control:
    The Ability to Internalize Responsibility 123
9. Perseverance:
    Dealing with Loss in the Best of All Possible Worlds.... 129
10. Godliness:
    Imitating God................................... 139
11. Kindness:
    The Power of Empathy 150
12. Love:
    The Centurion's Parallel........................... 159

Epilogue:
    According to What You Have Done 167
Readers' Guide 183
Bibliography 189
Notes 190

Preface

Beginning at the End

*L*et's begin at the end and work our way back to the present moment.

Heaven.

Most portrayals I've seen of this glorious, delightful, festive, sparkling, cheerful, happy place have been kind of cheesy.

Take, for instance, the portrayal in the movie *What Dreams May Come*. In this story, a virtuous doctor is killed in a car accident. When he arrives in heaven, he finds himself in a "painting" of his own creation, because in his earthly life he was passionate about his wife's art. In fact, according to the screenwriter, that's what heaven is like for everyone who is there: Each person creates a "heaven" that is a reflection of whatever brought him or her the greatest delight on earth. For some it's a playground. For others it is a never-ending game. God is somewhere off in the distance—aware of what's going on but not really engaged with anyone.

Another interesting portrayal of the final resting place is given in the book *The Five People You Meet in Heaven*. This tells the story of Eddie, an amusement park maintenance man who's tragically killed while trying to save a little girl from an out-of-control ride. Eddie's assignment in the afterlife is to speak with five people who will help him make peace with certain lifelong struggles that he had. Eddie finds himself in five different versions of heaven, each the unique and particular creation of the person residing there: a wedding, a beach, a diner, a brook, the amusement park where Eddie died.[1]

When I view these portrayals and even others that try to express Christian worldviews, I'm left feeling a bit empty. Each of the recently departed just seems to be creating his or her own version of heaven. I usually say to myself, "That's nice, but is that it?" So what do we do with all the treasure we've stored up in heaven? Just look at it? What are we actually going to be *doing*? There's *always* something missing.

Why are these depictions of paradise usually like that? Why is it that, with all the imaginative writing and spectacular special effects available to us, we cannot come up with a decent representation of the afterlife? Is there a theological reason behind this?

I think Solomon provides an answer for us in the book of Ecclesiastes: "[God] has ... set eternity in the hearts of men; yet they cannot fathom what God has done from beginning to end" (3:11). In other words, we can understand the idea that, somehow, we can live forever by doing something significant and meaningful, but we're never going to *fully comprehend how* in this life.

> [Christians], at their best, know that often they don't know. They do not have all the answers. They do not have God in their pocket. We cannot answer every question that any bright boy in the back row might ask. We have only light enough to walk by.[2]

In the New Testament, the apostle Paul concurs by quoting Isaiah: "No eye has seen, no ear has heard, no mind has conceived what God has prepared for those who love him" (1 Cor. 2:9; see Isa. 64:4). This means that any fictional account of heaven, no matter how brilliantly descriptive it is (and including any of the versions you'll find in this

PREFACE: BEGINNING AT THE END

book), is going to fall short of the real thing. On the other hand, we have many biblical descriptions of heaven, the most detailed of which is found in the last book of the New Testament.

Of course, that clears everything up, right? There's probably no other book of the Bible that enjoys more *universal agreement in interpretation* among Christians than Revelation. (I promise—that's as sarcastic as I'm going to get.)

There is obviously a wide variety of beliefs among Christians about the kingdom of God and how it will eventually manifest itself. These beliefs usually fall under a theological category called "eschatology" or the "doctrine of last things."

This book, while primarily about what our lives will be like after Christ returns, is *not* dependent upon any particular eschatology. What is *generally* agreed among Christians is that the kingdom of God has a *current* manifestation and will have a *future* manifestation. In this book we will often tap into Daniel's term for the kingdom of God, namely "his dominion" (Dan. 4:34; 6:26; 7:14). The present version we'll call the "Advancing Dominion," and the future version, the "Final Dominion." Of course, any manifestations of the kingdom could rightly be called the "Eternal Dominion."

No matter how a person understands the concept of the kingdom of God, whether in its present reality or in its future manifestation, Jesus' parables about the kingdom help us to understand these three universal truths:

1. The "Advancing Dominion" is passionately moving forward and fiercely opposed. In this regard, each of us is in one of three positions: "outside of," "not far from," or "entered into" the kingdom.
2. The "Final Dominion" will be a supernatural, exponential version of our present reality. Many of our experiences in this life will parallel similar experiences in the age to come.

3. Heavenly rewards are best described as types and levels of responsibility in the "Final Dominion"—positions of dedication and authority that are ultimately a reflection of how much God trusts each of us. This level of divine confidence will be lovingly revealed in what is known as "The Bema" or the judgment seat of Christ.

The challenge will be learning how to understand these rewards in light of grace. In order to do that, we need to grasp the idea that God's willingness to trust us and the incomprehensible depth of his love for us are *two very different things*.

GRACE AND PANCAKES

I have long struggled with the tension between grace and this time of evaluation, which seems to be based on the concept of gained trust. This struggle really hit me during the crisis in Atlanta when Brian Nichols apparently shot a judge and three others and held Ashley Smith hostage in her apartment. He allegedly tied her up and made her wait in the bathroom while he showered. Then they watched the TV news accounts of what he was doing.

After awhile, Nichols put his gun under a bed and untied Smith—then she made him pancakes. He was overwhelmed by the gesture.

That's grace.

However, while Smith was talking to Nichols, she didn't water down what lay ahead of him in regard to accountability for his deeds. She told him, in essence, "If you don't give up, you're probably going to die," or "Yes, you're going to prison, but you may discover God's purpose for you when you're there." When Nichols did give up, he did so peacefully.[3]

But when Nichols appeared before the judge, he was surrounded by no less than eight well-armed officers.[4] While he was the grateful recipient of someone's grace, he had purportedly done several horrible things and could not be trusted. Even though the depth of God's love for every living soul is beyond human comprehension, he still trusts some more than he does others.

Smith felt that she had been appointed by God to be there to mediate that crisis. Most of what we do in this life seems to be in preparation for something else. Is God getting us ready for something far bigger than we could ever accomplish in this earthly existence? Is this the true source of our significance and purpose in this life? Why does God seem to care so much about our fruitfulness and productivity? What is he looking for if we fail to be fruitful and productive, either due to human weakness or plain sinfulness? Perhaps instead of emphasizing the importance of how much each of us trusts God, we should ask, "How much does God trust me?" or "With what is he willing to trust me?"

According to What We Have Done

The Scriptures tell us repeatedly that we each will be rewarded according to what we have done.

> One thing God has spoken, two things have I heard: that you, O God, are strong, and that you, O Lord, are loving. Surely you will reward each person *according to what he has done*. (Ps. 62:11–12)

> For the Son of Man is going to come in his Father's glory with his angels, and then he will reward each person *according to what he has done*. (Matt. 16:27)

> God "will give to each person *according to what he has done*." (Rom. 2:6)

> And I saw the dead, great and small, standing before the throne, and books were opened. Another book was opened, which is the book of life. The dead were judged *according to what they had done* as recorded in the books. The sea gave up the dead that were in it, and death and Hades gave up the

dead that were in them, and each person was judged *according to what he had done*. (Rev. 20:12–13)

Behold, I am coming soon! My reward is with me, and I will give to everyone *according to what he has done*. (Rev. 22:12)

Does not he who weighs the heart perceive it? Does not he who guards your life know it? Will he not repay each person *according to what he has done*? (Prov. 24:12)

According to what you have done ...

after you sinned
after you failed
while you suffered
while you recovered
while you succeeded
while you rested

As we will see, all of these situations are opportunities for us to influence God's willingness to trust us—and to reward us accordingly.

As we move from the unfathomable mystery of the eternal to the tangible reality of what's happening to us at this very moment, things will get a little clearer each step of the way.

So let's begin.

Chapter 1

The Final Dominion:
Humans Ruling Where Angels Fear to Tread

> To myself I seem to have been only a boy playing on the seashore, and diverting myself in now and then finding a smoother pebble or a prettier shell than ordinary, while the great ocean of truth lay all undiscovered before me.
>
> Isaac Newton

The Reverend Jack Arnold, sixty-nine, was coming to the end of his sermon about heaven on a beautiful Sunday morning in January. As he was concluding this message, he paused, looked up briefly, and then fell to the floor. Doctors in the congregation attempted to revive him, but they were unable. Apparently the minister died instantly of cardiac arrest. "We were stunned," the associate pastor said. "It was traumatic, but how wonderful it was he died in his own church among the people he loved the most."

According to his sermon notes, this faithful pastor had intended to conclude his message with this passage:

> Jesus said to them, "I tell you the truth, at the renewal of all things, when the Son of Man sits on his glorious throne, you who have followed me will also sit on twelve thrones, judging the twelve tribes of Israel. And everyone who has left houses or brothers or sisters or father or mother or

children or fields for my sake will receive a hundred times as much and will inherit eternal life." (Matt. 19:28–29)

What Jesus was referring to in these verses ("the renewal of all things") is what I am calling the "Final Dominion." Again, almost every Christian eschatology ends in the same way, with the Son of God sitting on his throne, finally and forever unopposed.

What do we know about this time?

Randy Alcorn has written what I believe to be the definitive book on what the Bible says about the subject. It is aptly titled *Heaven*. Again, no human work is going adequately describe eternity, but the Bible gives us more than an inkling of what to expect—enough to motivate us to move forward and toward God.

In his book, Alcorn reminds us of many of the commonly known aspects about this supernatural realm:

1. Heaven is a place that actually *exists*. It is not a figurative destination or just symbolic of some greater virtue.
2. Heaven is a place of rest, where those who have been reconciled with God cease their earthly labors.
3. Heaven is a place of worship, where God is unceasingly praised for his power, glory, majesty, benevolence, and an infinite number of expressions of his divine attributes that will never be fully exhausted.

Alcorn also reminds of lesser-known aspects of heaven, as they are described in the Scriptures:

1. Heaven is described as a city, a place of multiple residences, subject to a central government. The city's gates are always open, and people will apparently travel in and out of it. The city does not represent the whole of heaven but remains at its core.

2. Heaven's labor will be refreshing, productive, and unthwarted, without futility and frustration, perhaps similar to what life in the garden of Eden was like prior to the fall.
3. Heaven is a place where the reconciled rule, a place where they hold positions of trust, responsibility, duty, effort, and the creative ability to lead and to do their work well.[1]

It is to the biblical truths of these last points about heavenly rulers, powers, authority, and duty that we now turn our attention.

Judging Angels

The Corinthians were a group of feisty Christians who the apostle Paul loved very deeply. But, spiritually speaking, they were like rebellious adolescents who were in constant need of loving correction and redirection.

One of those areas needing Paul's loving correction concerned lawsuits between believers. Apparently they were suing one another over frivolous matters in front of the secular courts and, in doing so, giving the church a bad name. Jesus gave ample authority to church leaders to resolve most, if not all, conflicts between Christians. In fact, today many vibrant mediation ministries, based on Jesus' principles of discipline and redemption, can help believers not only avoid costly litigation but also keep the doors open for reconciliation.

But apparently the Corinthians were ignoring these principles and embarrassing one another in front of judges whom they should have been trying to win for Christ. When rebuking the Corinthians for not dealing with this issue themselves, Paul made a rather enigmatic statement: "Do you not know that we will judge angels?" (1 Cor. 6:3).

What was Paul talking about? Will these everyday laypeople in the Corinthian church be judging *fallen* angels? Wasn't God going to take care of that at the final judgment? Were they going to be judging angels who remained loyal to God? If so, what would those angels be judged for if, in fact, they could not do anything that would dishonor God?

The mystery of what occurs in the invisible realms around us is just that: a mystery. As we've already discussed, there have been loads of movies and novels created about the interactions of angels, demons, and humans that all seem to fall short of credibility.

POSITIONS OF AUTHORITY

However, the Bible gives us an idea, even if it's just a little peek, about the positions of authority that angelic beings currently hold—places of authority, or ones like it, that perhaps one day glorified human beings will be assigned.

> *Has this world been so kind to you that you should leave with regret? There are better things ahead than any we leave behind.*
>
> —C. S. LEWIS

His intent was that now, through the church, the manifold wisdom of God should be made known to the rulers and authorities in the heavenly realms. (Eph. 3:10)

Apparently there are things that the rulers and authorities in the heavenly realms did not understand before the church was created by God. God's intention was to teach these powerful beings something about himself that they did not know before.

For our struggle is not against flesh and blood, but against the rulers, against the authorities, against the powers of this dark world and against the spiritual forces of evil in the heavenly realms. (Eph. 6:12)

Kingdom Spotlight

WHAT CAN WE LEARN FROM JOB'S PROLOGUE?

In the prologue to Job, an interesting, almost incidental comment reveals how the heavenly hierarchies operate:

> One day the angels came to present themselves before the LORD, and Satan also came with them. The LORD said to Satan, "Where have you come from?" Satan answered the LORD, "From roaming through the earth and going back and forth in it." (1:6–7)

At first it seems as if Satan doesn't really want to be there. I can imagine the interaction paralleled the lines of a frustrated parent trying to wring information from a less-than-enthusiastic teenager. "What did you do today?" "Nothing." "Where'd you go?" "Nowhere."

And then God started pushing a button. It seems that the Lord is not above comparing one of his servants above another. God decided to mention Job and how well he was doing. Perhaps the implied message was, "Here is a man who has far less than I ever gave you, yet you rebelled, and he remains faithful." This brought Satan out of his mumbling state and got him really angry.

> Have you not put a hedge around him and his household and everything he has? You have blessed the work of his hands, so that his flocks and herds are spread throughout the land. But stretch out your hand and strike everything he has, and he will surely curse you to your face. (vv. 10–11)

What did Satan do here? He pitched an idea.

In the publishing industry, thousands of book and article ideas get pitched every day (which makes me think, sometimes, that Satan is still at it, trying to sell certain "proposals"). Writers are pitching to editors, editors are pitching to publishing boards, publicists are pitching to media outlets, and so forth. Every few seconds, someone, somewhere, is pitching an idea. That's the nature of the creative process: Keep sending ideas up the flagpole to see if anyone salutes. And if the right people do salute, then you're that much closer to bringing the idea to life.

Satan, in an obviously rebellious state, suggested something that would ultimately be destructive, because that's what his irredeemable nature compels him to do. One has to wonder, though, if loyal angels pitch more creative, God-honoring ideas—and if one day glorified human beings will do the same.

There are obviously angelic beings who currently hold power in the heavenly realms but do not honor God with their authority and resist the advancement of God's kingdom—which would include your involvement in it.

> The angels who did not keep their positions of authority but abandoned their own home—these he has kept in darkness, bound with everlasting chains for judgment on the great Day. (Jude v. 6)

At least in the angelic realm, positions of authority can be lost just as easily as they were granted. It reminds me of the Lord's response to Pilate when the Roman procurator asserted his authority over Jesus' life: "You would have no power over me if it were not given to you from above" (John 19:11). Pilate eventually did lose his position of authority (he was removed from office by Vitellius, the legate of Syria), a volatile post in the Roman Empire he was so desperate to save that he allowed an innocent man to be crucified.

> [Jesus] has gone into heaven and is at God's right hand—with angels, authorities and powers in submission to him. (1 Peter 3:22)

> One day the angels came to present themselves before the LORD, and Satan also came with them. (Job 1:6)

> For by him all things were created: things in heaven and on earth, visible and invisible, whether thrones or powers or rulers or authorities; all things were created by him and for him. (Col. 1:16)

God has a purpose for creating this type of authoritative structure in the heavenly realms, where some created beings apparently have more authority than others. And if one day believers will judge angels, it follows that they will have greater authority and responsibility than those angelic beings.

Let's consider passages that seem to indicate that glorified human beings will hold positions of dedication and authority in the heavenly realms.

> Do you not know that the saints will judge the world? And if you are to judge the world, are you not competent to judge trivial cases? Do you not know that we will judge angels? How much more the things of this life! (1 Cor. 6:2–3)

> I saw thrones on which were seated those who had been given authority to judge. (Rev. 20:4)

> So that you may eat and drink at my table in my kingdom and sit on thrones, judging the twelve tribes of Israel. (Luke 22:30)

The meaning of "judging the twelve tribes of Israel" has significant eschatological implications that are beyond the scope of this book. What is important here, for our purposes, is that the Scriptures seem to indicate that glorified human beings will be eligible to hold some degree of authority in the heavenly realm. So, regardless of when it happens on the eschatological time line (whichever one proves to be the most accurate), this is what it will mean to reign with Christ:

> Blessed and holy are those who have part in the first resurrection. The second death has no power over them, but they will be priests of God and of Christ and will reign with him for a thousand years. (Rev. 20:6)

> If we endure, we will also reign with him. (2 Tim. 2:12)

POSSESSORS OF AUTHORITY

If glorified human beings will eventually hold positions of authority and devotion in heavenly realms, what will determine who holds those positions?

That is the question this book will attempt to answer. There's no need to flip to the last page—I'll give you the conclusion right here: Degrees of responsibility and reward in the heavenly realms will be awarded on the basis of how much God trusts each person with whom he has been reconciled.

This is what Jesus taught in his parables that could be titled "The Boss Who Goes Away and Comes Back."

The gospels of Matthew and Luke include a story that Jesus told to illustrate that there would be hierarchies of responsibility in his post-return dominion—and how he will determine who does what.

While we can infer from many Bible passages that God rewards according to the depth of our relationships with him, this parable offers the most detailed biblical basis for claiming that the degrees of heavenly rewards and responsibility are a reflection of God's willingness to trust us.

> While they were listening to this, he went on to tell them a parable, because he was near Jerusalem and the people thought that the kingdom of God was going to appear at once. He said: "A man of noble birth went to a distant country to have himself appointed king and then to return. So he called ten of his servants and gave them ten minas. 'Put this money to work,' he said, 'until I come back.'
>
> "But his subjects hated him and sent a delegation after him to say, 'We don't want this man to be our king.'
>
> "He was made king, however, and returned home. Then he sent for the servants to whom he had given the money, in order to find out what they had gained with it.
>
> "The first one came and said, 'Sir, your mina has earned ten more.'

"'Well done, my good servant!' his master replied. 'Because you have been trustworthy in a very small matter, take charge of ten cities.'

"The second came and said, 'Sir, your mina has earned five more.'

"His master answered, 'You take charge of five cities.'

"Then another servant came and said, 'Sir, here is your mina; I have kept it laid away in a piece of cloth. I was afraid of you, because you are a hard man. You take out what you did not put in and reap what you did not sow.'

"His master replied, 'I will judge you by your own words, you wicked servant! You knew, did you, that I am a hard man, taking out what I did not put in, and reaping what I did not sow? Why then didn't you put my money on deposit, so that when I came back, I could have collected it with interest?'

"Then he said to those standing by, 'Take his mina away from him and give it to the one who has ten minas.'

"'Sir,' they said, 'he already has ten!'

"He replied, 'I tell you that to everyone who has, more will be given, but as for the one who has nothing, even what he has will be taken away. But those enemies of mine who did not want me to be king over them—bring them here and kill them in front of me.'" (Luke 19:11–27; see also Matt. 25:14–30)

In the context of this passage, the multitudes had been following Jesus and listening intently to his teaching. Just prior to this, Jesus had his reconciling encounter with Zacchaeus, one of the most despised men in Jerusalem (because he was a tax collector for the Romans). Perhaps the presence of Zacchaeus, and what he represented, caused the people to reflect upon the oppressive occupying force that resided there.

Ever since the fall of Judah to Babylon in 586 BC, the Jewish people had been in exile. Yes, they were able to return to their homeland under the leadership of Nehemiah and Ezra, but (in biblical times) they never

BRING IT ON

As in the heavenly realms, we also live in systems of hierarchy; they are not always benevolent, but they are tiered structures of authority all the same. Those higher in the hierarchy may have greater perks, but the burden of their responsibility is much greater.

To him whom much is given, much will be required. (See Luke 12:48.)

It is no small thing to be a CEO of a company and have the livelihoods of hundreds or thousands of people in your hands—not to mention the survival of the corporation. Of course, some executives have become completely insensitive to the burdens of those who work for them, but I believe that they are the exception. Besides, their companies are usually the first to fall. Watch any U.S. president progress through his four years, and in most cases you will see his hair gray prematurely, and you will see the strain in his eyes. But the good ones never give up or cave in to the relentless criticism.

---

really regained their independent status as a nation, much less the superpower status they had enjoyed under David and Solomon.

By the time Jesus appeared on the scene four hundred years later, this pseudonation had been through a lot, without any prophetic word from God, and had been ruled off and on by various powers. Of course, by the time Jesus arrived on the scene, the oppressor of the century was Rome.

As the Jews read the Hebrew Scriptures, they understood that a Messiah was on the way. In their minds, of course, this Messiah would be a political deliverer; like the judges of old, he would rise up and restore Israel to its former glory.

Some forty years after Jesus' earthly ministry, Rome put an end to the dream of a political messiah once and for all by destroying Jerusalem and its temple in AD 70. In the meantime, however, many Jews believed that Jesus was going to prevent anything of the sort from happening. In an attempt to correct their

To him whom much is given, much will be required.

I have seen some of those who have been given much handle it responsibly. These are people I aspire to be like. When confronted with the prospect of increased accountability, instead of shrinking back, they seem to say, "Let's do it!" They're ready to be evaluated at any time because they're constantly examining themselves. If there are gaps in their thinking or behavior, they want to know about them so they can be addressed. And the sooner they're revealed the better.

I believe these are the type of people Paul had in mind when he wrote, "But if we judged ourselves, we would not come under judgment" (1 Cor. 11:31).

To him whom much is given, much will be required.

Most of those who responsibly handle what they've been given would reply to that statement, "Bring it on!"

---

views, he told them the "The Boss Who Goes Away and Comes Back" parable to help them understand what the kingdom was going to be like.

In today's terms, the stewardship parable is about a venture capitalist who had entrusted several entrepreneurs with a certain amount of money. In fact, they all received the same amount of cash. A *mina* was a varying unit of currency that could be worth as much as three months' wages. So the servants not only had to live on this money but also had to invest according to the nobleman's explicit instructions.

Jesus clearly intended the people to identify the "man of noble birth" with him. Of course, after his crucifixion and resurrection, he was going to go away to become King:

> God exalted [Jesus] to the highest place and gave him the name that is above every name. (Phil. 2:9)

On his robe and on his [Jesus'] thigh he has this name written: KING OF KINGS AND LORD OF LORDS. (Rev. 19:16)

The subjects who rejected Jesus as King were, in the immediate context, the religious leaders of his day and, in the extended context, anyone who rejects Jesus' authority.

When the master returned, he called these servants to account. The most successful servant stepped forward first. His mina had earned ten more—he had turned three months' wages into nearly three years' wages.

[The master replied,] "Well done, my good servant! ... Because you have been trustworthy in a very small matter, take charge of ten cities." (Luke 19:17)

Ten cities! Can you imagine?

Let's say you received $15,000 to invest, and you put that money into three high-risk businesses, and after a certain amount of time, the original $15,000 was now worth $150,000. The person who gave you the money up front turned out to be much more powerful than you thought. And that person was very impressed. Because you had proved trustworthy with his money, he decided to put you in charge of his teams—namely those who were doing business in New York, Los Angeles, Chicago, Dallas, Memphis, Baltimore, Boston, Seattle, Minneapolis, and Orlando.

Of course, we could say that since these parables are metaphors, Jesus probably did not mean literal cities. But the parallel parable in Matthew 25 talks about the successful entrepreneurs being placed "in charge of many things" because, like their counterparts in Luke's parable, they were "trustworthy in a very small matter."

To be in charge of something, whether cities or projects, implies responsibility. And in the case of these parables, the degree of

MORE WILL BE GIVEN

You may have heard it said many times that if you want to get something done, ask the busiest person you know. Busy people tend to be energized and motivated and often find creative ways to get things done. Of course, frenetic activity does not always equate with productivity, but again, you can tell who's for real by the fruit that he or she bears.

Jesus seemed to illustrate this in the parable of the faithful stewards, in response to the master's command to give the mina of the faithless servant to the one who already has ten:

> Then he said to those standing by, "Take his mina away from him and give it to the one who has ten minas."
> "Sir," they said, "he already has ten!"
> He replied, "I tell you that to everyone who has, more will be given." (Luke 19:24–26)

The active, productive individual gets results. He or she may fail repeatedly, but if that is the case, this person constantly makes course corrections so the final result will be useful—especially to the one who assigned the task or those who will benefit from that person's efforts.

One might argue that Jesus is not primarily concerned with the even distribution of wealth, but rather with the proper allocation of resources that reflects his willingness to trust particular individuals.

---

responsibility is a reflection of trustworthiness. No metaphor there.

Of course, there was one servant in the parable who buried the money that had been given to him, and it didn't even gain interest. The consequences for him were harsh—but the punishment for those who did not want the nobleman to be king was even worse. The identity of those who "bury their talents" will be addressed later—but, for now suffice it to say, that passively "waiting for whatever God has for me" can be detrimental to your spiritual health.

THE HUMAN NEED TO BE TRUSTED

Most people want to be trusted. It's a part of our emotional makeup. True, there are con artists out there who build up trust in order to exploit others, but they seem to be the exception rather than the rule. Most people enjoy the feeling of being trusted, and some dread the possibility of letting people down.

Jesus often tapped into this deeply embedded emotional need to make his point:

> Whoever can be trusted with very little can also be trusted with much, and whoever is dishonest with very little will also be dishonest with much. So if you have not been trustworthy in handling worldly wealth, who will trust you with true riches? And if you have not been trustworthy with someone else's property, who will give you property of your own? (Luke 16:10–12)

One of the most effective ways to manage and motivate competent people is to clearly define the objectives of an important task and instruct them to use whatever abilities God has given them to make it happen.

Then make sure that you get out of their way.

As promised, we're moving from the end to the present moment. We have seen that the Final Dominion is essentially the same in any eschatology. Jesus has gone away, has been made King, and will one day return to his own. After he returns, there will be a time of perfectly accurate accounting, where it will be abundantly clear how much God is willing to trust each of those servants with whom he has been reconciled.

In the theological circles, this is often called the Bema Seat, or the judgment seat of Christ. To this loving but fiery time of evaluation we now turn our attention.

CHAPTER 2

PROTESTANT PURGATORY:
The Bema Seat Judgment

> My friend, do not wait for the last judgment,
> for it is occurring every day.
>
> Albert Camus

Catholic doctrine describes purgatory as a place where the departed soul undergoes a fiery process of cleansing in order to prepare for its eventual entrance into heaven. Dante made it famous in part 2, *Purgatory,* of his *Divine Comedy.* According to Catholic belief, a person's soul (upon departing from the body) undergoes an often long process of fiery cleansing—and, some would say, atonement—from the sins that he or she committed in his or her lifetime. Unlike hell, purgatory is not a place of abandonment and hopelessness. The soul knows that the process will end eventually with its glorious entrance into heaven.

At one point in church history, religious leaders abused the concept of purgatory. They taught that a soul's time in this fiery place could be significantly diminished with an appropriate contribution. A monk named Johann Tetzel coined a phrase to highlight this practice: "As soon as the coin in the coffer rings, a soul from purgatory springs."

C. S. Lewis believed in purgatory, but it was not the Catholic version, shaped by Dante, that we have come to know:

Mind you, the Reformers have good reasons for throwing doubt on the Romish doctrine concerning Purgatory as that Romish doctrine had become ... [but] our souls demand Purgatory, don't they? Would it not break the heart if God said to us, "It is true, my son, that your breath smells and your rags drip with mud and slime, but we are charitable here and no one will upbraid you with these things, nor draw away from you. Enter into the joy"? Should we not reply, "With submission, sir, and if there is no objection, I'd rather be cleaned first." "It may hurt, you know"—"Even so, sir."[1]

CLEANSING

I believe the cleansing process Lewis had in mind here is described to us by the apostle Paul in 1 Corinthians 3:11–15:

> No one can lay any foundation other than the one already laid, which is Jesus Christ. If any man builds on this foundation using gold, silver, costly stones, wood, hay or straw, his work will be shown for what it is, because the Day will bring it to light. It will be revealed with fire, and the fire will test the quality of each man's work. If what he has built survives, he will receive his reward. If it is burned up, he will suffer loss; he himself will be saved, but only as one escaping through the flames.

Biblically speaking, there's nothing atoning about this process. The person who has been reconciled with God by faith is cleansed from all sin by the blood of Christ. This is beyond dispute, as far as the teaching of historically orthodox Christianity is concerned. As C. S. Lewis said, "The Reformers have good reasons for throwing doubt" on this Catholic doctrine.[2] So for this reason we're calling what follows "Protestant Purgatory" because it does describe a spiritual cleansing that, humanly speaking, only lasts a few minutes—but has significant bearing on the roles and responsibilities that a person will be given in the Final Dominion.

And if there's loss, as Lewis implies, it's going to hurt.

I believe that most believers want to be in a state of absolute authenticity before God—to be able to see ourselves as God sees us, warts and all so that (1) we can understand the depth of God's compassion and grace for us and so that (2) we can, by God's grace and by the power of the Holy Spirit, do something about the warts as we become aware of their existence.

Granted, some will read this passage and say, "*So what* if it's all burned up? All I care about is getting in." For some this is merely the expression of an immature but saving faith. For others it is the ultimate in spiritual self-deception. To read this passage (or any biblical text) with indifference is an indication that something serious needs to be addressed in that person's heart.

> *Your Honor, a courtroom is a crucible. In it, we burn away irrelevancies until we're left with a pure product—the truth, for all time.*
>
> —CAPTAIN JEAN-LUC PICARD, STAR TREK: THE NEXT GENERATION

In 1 Corinthians 3:11–15, the apostle Paul describes a fiery process by which the earthly decisions, attitudes, and actions of Christians will be evaluated, and he describes how the results of that test will determine what eternity will be like for them. To help us understand this process, Paul used an analogy of a house built over a lifetime with the materials of a believer's choosing. This house is built on the foundation of faith.

If no such foundation exists—as it is in the case of those who choose not to be reconciled with God—there is a different evaluation. Based on passages like Jesus' sayings in Matthew 11—"But I tell you, it will be more bearable for Tyre and Sidon on the day of judgment than for you.... It will be more bearable for Sodom on the day of judgment than for you" (vv. 22, 24)—

IF THE EVIL MAN REPENTS

Unfortunately, the word *repentance* has become a bit watered down in our time. For some it means merely "to change one's mind." While this definition is literally true, repentance is so much more than this.

As I wrote about in *The Prayer of Revenge: Forgiveness in the Face of Injustice*, true repentance can be remembered by the initialism of ABCM. A person must first *A*, Acknowledge that he has done something that dishonors God; *B*, he must Bear the burden of his irresponsible behavior and take responsibility for the destructive consequences of his actions; *C*, he must do everything humanly possible to Correct the behavior; and then, *M*, if he fails in A, B, or C, he must desire reconciliation so much that he humbly asks for Mercy.

Ezekiel seemed to reflect this idea:

> And if I say to the wicked man, "You will surely die," but he then turns away from his sin and does what is just and right—if he gives back what he took in pledge for a loan, returns what he has stolen, follows the decrees that give life, and does no evil, he will surely live; he will

there will apparently be degrees of punishment in hell, depending on the depth of a person's contempt for the Holy One. The earthly indifference of those who want nothing to do with God will turn to blasphemous defiance when they finally stand before him. There will be no regrets, no repentance—only the embittered gnashing of teeth that reflects a heart utterly unwilling to internalize responsibility for anything that individual has done.

For people who have been reconciled with God, there clearly will be degrees of reward in heaven, and those rewards are best described as types and levels of responsibility in the Final Dominion. As mentioned previously, we understand this from biblical passages such as the parable of the faithful stewards in Luke 19, not die. None of the sins he has committed will be remembered against him. He has done what is just and right; he will surely live.... If a righteous man turns from his righteousness and does evil, he will die for it. And if a wicked man turns away from his wickedness and does what is just and right, he will live by doing so. Yet, O house of Israel, you say, "The way of the Lord is not just." But I will judge each of you *according to his own ways*. (33:14–20)

If the evil man repents, he will receive the reward of the good that he was seeking, the good that he previously twisted into an abusive action—but then regretted. For example: The man who spent his life with prostitutes, seeking an illusive intimacy, will be given the security of genuine intimacy—if he repents of his evil. The once power-hungry CEO will be given leadership responsibilities, not in order to dominate and control his subordinates (as he did before), but to accomplish his commander's objectives—if he repents of his evil. Ultimately, whatever sense of "security" the sinful person was pursuing by disobeying God will be given to him—if he repents.

in which the master says to his servants, "Because you have been trustworthy in a very small matter, take charge of ten cities" (v. 17), or a similar parable in Matthew 25 where he says, "Well done, good and faithful servant! You have been faithful with a few things; I will put you in charge of many things" (v. 23). The criteria for these assignments will not necessarily be based on how much we trust God, but rather on how much, and with what, he is willing to trust us—and this is what will be revealed in the cleansing fires of the judgment seat of Christ.

Even though believers are saved by grace, apparently it's possible to suffer loss at heaven's door based on some of the low-quality "materials" that we may have chosen. If we choose wisely, our "building materials" will survive the test of fire, and we will be rewarded accordingly—again, with responsibilities that reflect the choices we've made in life.

As our knowledge of this process grows, we gain an increased sense of significance and purpose in our lives. We begin to sense that God is preparing us for something far, far bigger than we've ever imagined.

Theologians have called this the Bema Seat Judgment, named after a first-century platform called the "Bema Seat" that often served as a place of judgment and evaluation. Pontius Pilate probably declared Jesus innocent of the charges against him from such a platform.

Thus, we might call the passage in 1 Corinthians 3:11–15 a description of the Bema *House*—the figurative structure that represents the spiritual quality of a Christian's life.

Of course, there are many ways to measure that quality: the genuine depths of one's love, faith, hope, or compassion. In this book, the criterion will be God's trust. Again, not how much we trusted God (which, in itself, is very important), but how much he trusts each person who goes through this fiery trial.

According to the apostle Paul, every Christian must choose the materials with which to build his or her "Bema House"—"gold, silver, precious stones, wood, hay, stubble" (1 Cor. 3:12 KJV). What does each of these materials represent in the life of the Christian? Can we determine *now* how much of our Bema House will be standing after it's subjected to God's loving but fiery process of evaluation? Can we trade materials, even in the middle of construction, if we find them to be more porous than precious?

How do we reconcile the evaluation of works with the clear teaching of the Scriptures that we are saved by grace alone? Is it possible to lose God's trust without losing his love?

To answer these questions, we'll take a closer look at this passage and others like it in the Scriptures that help us fill out this allegorical picture. But before we do that, let's wrestle a bit with this question: Is it wrong to be motivated by reward?

What Motivates You?

There are two basic human motivations:

1. The fear of loss
2. The anticipation of reward

While it seems crass to be motivated by either of these things, one has to wonder if it can really be any other way. Biblically speaking, clearly God uses both punishment and compensation to incentivize people.

Loss or Punishment

G. K. Chesterton once said that the doctrine of original sin was the only Christian doctrine for which we have any empirical evidence.[3] Ask any parent, and he or she will quickly tell you how the bent toward rebellion usually shows up at a very early age in children—usually around eighteen to twenty-four months (they're not called the "terrible twos" for nothing). And clearly the way to keep those rebellious, sinful tendencies in check is by imposing the fear of loss, like we do with those bothersome time-outs that accompany loving discipline.

For many adults, it's difficult to accept the prospect of being disciplined for anything. For some us this holds true when we're pulled over by a police officer for an *alleged* traffic violation. The word *alleged* is emphasized here because that's usually our first reaction: *There must be some mistake.*

During my college years, I delivered pizzas to earn some extra money. One night, I was traveling down a four-lane road with a mobile oven in the passenger seat, and I was going about forty-two miles per hour. Within about three blocks of my destination, the inside of my car was suddenly filled with flashing red and blue light. Again, my first reaction was to think, *There must be some mistake.*

The officer was very polite and informed me that I was speeding. Thinking that the speed limit was forty miles per hour on this huge road, I thought he was being a little strict. Of course, all kinds of things you'd like to say go through your mind at a time like that: "I thought you had to be physically fit to be a cop" or "Are you Andy or Barney?"

But, of course, I kept my mouth shut and even thanked the officer when he handed me the ticket—and then I thought, *Why did you do that? Isn't this humiliating enough?*

Well, I delivered the pizza and started back to the restaurant. During the trip, with my eyes checking the speedometer every five seconds, I was determined to fight this ticket. I was going to take pictures to determine where the speed limit sign was in relation to where I was pulled over. And I could probably substantiate the claim that certain police radars have a margin of error around plus or minus three miles per hour, which would, of course, be enough reasonable doubt to get me off the hook.

In addition, a few friends told me that if the officer didn't show up on the court date, I'd be off the hook automatically, so it's *always* worth fighting a ticket. (Note: The only thing that's *always* worth doing, in cases like these, is taking the legal advice of nonlawyers with a grain of salt.)

I dutifully arrived on the court date, ready to do battle. It turned out that this officer had also ticketed about twenty other people, who were ahead of me in the courtroom. And he was there too, apparently to guarantee that no one would wiggle out of one of his tickets.

As I heard case after case before mine, my hopes of vindication gradually diminished. By the time the DA got to mine, he was quite irritated with all these blatantly guilty people trying to get out of their just punishment. He seemed ready to throw the book at me. He had the still-polite officer spend about fifteen minutes presenting documents on how well calibrated his radar was. Margin of error? One mile per hour. So much for that defense. Number of miles per hour over the speed limit? Twelve, not two. Whoops. The speed limit in that area was thirty miles per hour, not forty. My case was crumbling by the minute. By the time the judge asked if I had anything to say in my defense, the best I could conjure up was a weak "Nope."

For my impudence the DA wanted to double my fine and have me cover the day's court costs—not just mine. Mercifully, the judge said that since this was my first offense, and obviously the first and last time I was going to contest this sort of thing, he let me go with a modified fee. And, for some reason, it ended up being only a third of the original fine. But I learned my lesson.

Being disciplined as an adult is obviously a pride-shattering experience. When it comes to being disciplined for spiritually related matters, Jesus set up a process for church discipline in Matthew 18:15–19. The process is intended to caringly confront and redeem believers who are doing reckless or immoral things. Many people think that church discipline has

EMBARRASSED AT THE JUDGMENT SEAT OF CHRIST

A well-known Christian leader once commented that he would feel utterly betrayed by God if the Lord were to reveal any of his sins at the judgment seat of Christ. He insisted that since God removed his sins "as far as the east is from the west" (Ps. 103:12), they should never come up—either in this life or the next. And for his sins to be revealed in front of everyone would simply be so embarrassing that he was not sure he could even forgive the Lord for doing such a thing.

I don't think the Lord owes us any freedom from embarrassment at the Bema Seat. The fact is, that which is hidden will be revealed, plain and simple (see Ps. 69:5; 1 Cor. 4:5). The person who has truly acknowledged his sin will not be embarrassed; on the contrary, he will be stunned at the depth of God's grace. If a believer is going to wait until the judgment seat of Christ to *finally* acknowledge what he has habitually hidden, then he deserves whatever awkwardness may result. Those who persevere will also be commended, with nothing to be embarrassed about (see 2 Tim. 2:12).

REWARDED ACCORDING TO DESIRE

What motivates you?

Each of us has God-given desires that we can use in ways that honor him or in ways that lose his trust. The fulfillment of these desires is what moves us in one direction or the other.

Dr. Steven Reiss, in a book called *Who Am I? The 16 Basic Desires That Motivate Our Actions and Define Our Personalities*, outlines sixteen basic desires that all human beings have to one degree or another. In fact, some are dominant, some are average, and some we can simply live without and never notice. According to Reiss, the particular mix of desires is what makes up the unique motivational pattern of the individual and determines how best to reward that person.

Here are the sixteen desires (or motivations) as outlined by Dr. Reiss:

Power—the desire to influence others
Independence—the desire for self-reliance
Curiosity—the desire for knowledge
Acceptance—the desire for inclusion
Order—the desire for organization

fallen by the wayside in recent days, but that simply is not true. Church discipline happens often, but it happens discreetly and behind the scenes so that most of the cases do not need to be taken before the congregation.

First Corinthians 3 describes a heavenly process in which disciplinary loss is possible, even though the individual is still saved "as one escaping through the flames" (v. 15). Our response to the possibility of this happening is similar to those feelings that we experience in regard to earthly matters. Even so, because loss and discipline hurt, the experience can legitimately be used as a source of motivation to find what our spiritual warts might be, then diligently seek to remove them.

Saving—the desire to collect things
Honor—the desire to be loyal to one's heritage
Idealism—the desire for social justice
Social contact—the desire for companionship
Family—the desire to look after children
Status—the desire for social standing
Justice—the desire to make things right
Romance—the desire for intimacy and beauty
Eating—the desire to consume food
Physical exercise—the desire to work out
Tranquility—the desire for emotional calm[4]

In terms of heavenly rewards, the idea of responsibility in the kingdom may appeal to the person who legitimately desires power and status. But there are many, many others who don't want to be "in charge" of anything. What about those who relish acceptance or tranquility? How will God reward them?

In ways that we may not fully understand right now, any heavenly reward will be geared to the person to whom it is given—namely, to his or her respective God-honoring desires.

Reward

And what about the flip side? If it's legitimate to pursue spiritual growth to avoid loss at the judgment seat of Christ, can we also be positively motivated to pursue growth because of the prospect of reward?

Many believers claim that they are not all that interested in heavenly rewards. After all, don't the twenty-four elders just hand back their crowns anyway (see Rev. 4:10)? For these fine folks, it's simply enough to be granted entrance into heaven and to hear the Lord say, "Well done, good and faithful servant!" (Matt. 25:21).

But do we dare *not* call that divine affirmation a reward?

Consider also some of these other passages from the Old and

New Testaments that seem to indicate God intends us to be driven by the prospect of compensation:

May the LORD repay you for what you have done. May you be richly rewarded by the LORD, the God of Israel, under whose wings you have come to take refuge. (Ruth 2:12)

The LORD rewards every man for his righteousness and faithfulness. (1 Sam. 26:23)

Then men will say, "Surely the righteous still are rewarded; surely there is a God who judges the earth." (Ps. 58:11)

Surely you will reward each person according to what he has done. (Ps. 62:12)

He who is kind to the poor lends to the LORD, and he will reward him for what he has done. (Prov. 19:17)

See, the Sovereign LORD comes with power, and his arm rules for him. See, his reward is with him, and his recompense accompanies him. (Isa. 40:10)

But I said, "I have labored to no purpose; I have spent my strength in vain and for nothing. Yet what is due me is in the LORD's hand, and my reward is with my God." (Isa. 49:4)

For I, the LORD, love justice; I hate robbery and iniquity. In my faithfulness I will reward them and make an everlasting covenant with them. (Isa. 61:8)

The LORD has made proclamation to the ends of the earth: "Say to the Daughter of Zion, 'See, your Savior comes! See, his reward is with him, and his recompense accompanies him.'" (Isa. 62:11)

KINGDOM SPOTLIGHT

TO WHAT EXTENT DOES GOD RULE?

Much debate has raged over the current extent of God's influence over the world. Remember when Satan was tempting Jesus in the wilderness and showed him all the kingdoms of the world? Satan claimed they were his to give, a claim Jesus neither confirmed nor denied.

However, Jesus knew that one day Satan would be defeated and that his Father, in turn, would give his Son those kingdoms. In order for that to happen, however, there could be no shortcuts. Jesus chose the path of obedience.

In any case, the Scriptures are clear about the extent of God's current reign:

> Hezekiah prayed to the LORD: "O LORD, God of Israel, enthroned between the cherubim, you alone are God over all the kingdoms of the earth." (2 Kings 19:15, see Isa. 37:16)

> The LORD has established his throne in heaven, and his kingdom rules over all. (Ps. 103:19)

God currently rules over all the kingdoms of the world, even though not all acknowledge his sovereignty.

I the LORD search the heart and examine the mind, to reward a man according to his conduct, according to what his deeds deserve. (Jer. 17:10)

Rejoice and be glad, because great is your reward in heaven, for in the same way they persecuted the prophets who were before you. (Matt. 5:12)

Your Father, who sees what is done in secret, will reward you. (Matt. 6:4)

For the Son of Man is going to come in his Father's glory with his angels, and then he will reward each person according to what he has done. (Matt. 16:27)

You know that the Lord will reward everyone for whatever good he does. (Eph. 6:8)

CROWNS

Biblical rewards are often described as "crowns":

Everyone who competes in the games goes into strict training. They do it to get a crown that will not last; but we do it to get a crown that will last forever. (1 Cor. 9:25)

Now there is in store for me the crown of righteousness, which the Lord, the righteous Judge, will award to me on that day—and not only to me, but also to all who have longed for his appearing. (2 Tim. 4:8)

Blessed is the man who perseveres under trial, because when he has stood the test, he will receive the crown of life that God has promised to those who love him. (James 1:12)

Do not be afraid of what you are about to suffer. I tell you, the devil will put some of you in prison to test you, and you will suffer persecution for ten days. Be faithful, even to the point of death, and I will give you the crown of life. (Rev. 2:10)

Without faith it is impossible to please God, because anyone who comes to him must believe that he exists and that he rewards those who earnestly seek him. (Heb. 11:6)

Behold, I am coming soon! My reward is with me, and I will give to everyone according to what he has done. (Rev. 22:12)

And, of course, the 1 Corinthians 3 passage speaks unapologetically of reward.

To settle the "motivated by reward" question, let's ask, "What motivated Christ?"

Quite often in the movies we witness moments of import as a crown is lowered onto an individual's head. If the recipient is a villain, we fear how he or she will misuse the authority that the crown represents. If the recipient is a hero, we anticipate that the character will do courageous things with his newly endowed powers.

Throughout ancient history, crowns have been symbols of authority and responsibility, much like the purpose that stars and other medals serve in the military. (When running onto the battlefield, you can easily tell an officer's rank by the insignia on his or her lapel, hat, or shoulders.) Egyptian crowns were often of different heights in order to designate degrees of honor and responsibility.

When the elders lay their crowns at the feet of Jesus in Revelation, it signifies their acknowledgment that all authority is derived from him. One is reminded of Jesus' statement to his enemy Pontius Pilate: "You would have no authority unless it was given to you from above" (see John 19:11). Though the Scriptures do not say so, Jesus will probably give the elders their crowns back, expecting them to exercise the authority and responsibility that those symbols of God-honoring power represent.

Let us fix our eyes on Jesus, the author and perfecter of our faith, *who for the joy set before him* endured the cross, scorning its shame, and sat down at the right hand of the throne of God. (Heb. 12:2)

Jesus looked ahead *to the prize that was meaningful to him* to get him through a terrifying and humiliating experience.

These two motivations—the fear of loss and prospect of reward—are brought together in John's second epistle when he writes:

Watch out that you do not lose what you have worked for, but that you may be rewarded fully. (v. 8)

"Watch[ing] out," looking for the spiritual blind spots that might create loss at heaven's door, and strengthening the gifts and desires of our hearts move us toward storing up for ourselves treasure in heaven.

So, yes, it is clearly legitimate to be motivated by the fear of loss and the prospect of reward. We certainly see this in our earthly experience, and it's no different as we make our way toward heaven. Sure, a few people do what they do only because they don't want to lose what they have. They show up to work because they'd get fired otherwise. They stay faithful to their spouses only because they don't want to experience the turmoil of divorce. They go to church because they don't want to suffer the disapproval of their pastors and friends.

But the vast majority of believers want to do a good job, want to please the Lord, want to work for the kingdom because of the prospect of earthly and heavenly rewards. And, sure, those rewards may have tangible expressions (like jewels in our crowns or rooms in our mansions), but they will only be outward manifestations of what really matters, and that is the extent to which God is willing to trust us.

Shortly after explaining the Bema Seat Judgment to the believers in Corinth, Paul wanted to make something crystal clear to them: There was something they could do *now* to affect what would happen to them on the day: "If we judged ourselves, we would not come under judgment" (1 Cor. 11:31).

And this is the purpose of this book: to walk through the process of self-evaluation so we don't have to worry about loss at Jesus' feet, to take a look at the biblically mandated things that we can do to affect our reward—namely, the depth of God's willingness to trust us.

Chapter 3

Peter's Vocational Test for Kingdom Placement:
Characteristics of the Person God Trusts

Love all, trust a few.

William Shakespeare

Nowhere in the history of the church have Christians shown more imagination than when it comes to coming up with interesting allegorical interpretations of difficult-to-understand Bible passages. Of course, understanding what Paul meant by "gold, silver, precious stones, wood, hay, [and] stubble" (1 Cor 3:12 KJV) is no exception.

A few years ago, I was invited to a dinner discussion with about 150 Muslims, Jews, and Christians in attendance. What initially struck me as odd about this gathering was that I could not tell who belonged to what group until each person started articulating his or her beliefs. Even some of those with apparent ethnic connections belonged to a different group than I had assumed.

One of the first people to speak at our table was an apparently well-seasoned orator. About two sentences into his diatribe, I realized that this man was a Christian, and a preacher at that.

Although I did not see how his point connected to what we were talking about, he insisted that the supreme biblical basis for

> **Y**ears ago I heard Warren Wiersbe, former pastor of Moody Church and author of the Be series, talk about the dove that Noah released from the ark. He said, "We see this dove flying throughout the Old Testament looking for someone on whom to land. It comes to Abraham and says, 'I cannot land on him—he lied about his wife.' It comes to Isaac and says, 'I cannot land on him—he lied about his wife.' Then it comes to Jacob and says, 'I cannot land on him—he lied about everything.' So it goes for thousands of years until at last it comes to rest on the shoulder of Jesus, the sinless one, of whom the Father says, 'This is my beloved Son; in him I am well pleased.'"
>
> I think that is great imagery, imaginatively pulling together Noah's dove and the Holy Spirit at Jesus' baptism. Of course, no one thinks Wiersbe really means that it's the same dove. It is just a helpful picture designed to convey spiritual truth.
>
> —Paul Lundquist, pastor

unity in the church was the seamless garment of Christ that the Roman soldiers refused to divide among themselves. Like the seamless garment, Christians needed to portray an undivided, united front to the world. That was certainly food for thought, as well as an interesting illustration, but did the gospel writer really want his readers to make that connection?

Hidden Truth

Allegory can be creatively used as a teaching tool, as long as everyone understands that the interpreter is not conveying his illustration as either divine revelation or the intention of the biblical writer—unless, of course, the biblical writer plainly interpreted the analogy. For example, Jesus plainly interpreted the meaning of the elements in the parable of the sower and the seed: "Listen then to what the parable of the sower means" (Matt. 13:18).

Quite often, the biblical writers referred to a Bible story and gave us a new allegorical interpretation of the passage. The apostle Paul told us that Sarah and Hagar (Abraham's wife and Sarah's handmaiden) represented the old and new covenants. If an inspired biblical writer has given us such an interpretation, then, of course, we must take it at face value. It is as divinely inspired as the original story.

When Albert Schweitzer wrote his famous book *The Quest of the Historical Jesus*, he criticized his predecessors by saying that all they had done was to look down a well and, seeing their own reflection, proclaim, "Behold, this historical Jesus," when, in fact, they were simply describing an idealized version of themselves.[1] Then Schweitzer went on to do exactly the same thing in his book.

We want to avoid the same error. By defining what we think Paul meant by "gold, silver, precious stones, wood, hay, stubble" (1 Cor. 3:12 KJV), we're revealing what we consider to be the contrast between the futile and the fruitful Christian life. And since those of us who are teachers will be held to a stricter judgment, this is something we in particular need to approach with solemnity and humility.

Allegorical interpretation of Scripture attempts to find a deeper, more spiritual meaning beyond the literal words on the page. The church fathers Clement and Origen started us down this path, but soon things appeared to get out of hand. Even Eustathius (ca. 270–360), bishop of Antioch, criticized Origen on his freewheeling use of allegory. For example, Origen had claimed that when the witch of Endor called up Samuel, the event was *intended* to foreshadow Christ's resurrection. Eustathius, as reverently and piously as possible, said that this was hogwash and that neither the biblical writer nor the Holy Spirit intended such a connection.[2]

All this is to say that we need to be careful when we're looking at a passage like 1 Corinthians 3:15, where Paul used obvious metaphors like "gold, silver, precious stones, wood, hay, [and] stubble" (1 Cor. 3:12 KJV). We must not come right out and say, "Paul meant gold to represent this and silver to represent this, wood to represent this, etc." If he had used these metaphors in another context and defined them, perhaps we could draw an exact parallel, but he did not.

The closest he came is 2 Timothy 2:20:

> In a large house there are articles not only of gold and silver, but also of wood and clay; some are for noble purposes and some for ignoble.

In this passage, Paul said that these materials represent significance of purpose, but he did not define what those purposes are. However, this could still be valuable in our interpretation of the 1 Corinthians passage; whatever the materials represent, they represent "things" of increasing or decreasing values.

There are other Old Testament passages that also lend themselves to this idea:

> All King Solomon's goblets were gold, and all the household articles in the Palace of the Forest of Lebanon were pure gold. Nothing was made of silver, because silver was considered of little value in Solomon's days. (1 Kings 10:21)

> Instead of bronze I will bring you gold, and silver in place of iron. Instead of wood I will bring you bronze, and iron in place of stones. I will make peace your governor and righteousness your ruler. (Isa. 60:17)

So what are we to do with this passage? What was Paul's intention?

It's safe to say that Paul intended a progressive quality to our "building materials" that is to be revealed by the gracious but fiery evaluative process of God.

If Paul meant to say that those "building materials" were either good or bad, he would have limited himself to two substances. For

> The allegorical method attempts to overcome the difficulties of morally perplexing Biblical passages and to harmonize them with certain traditions and accepted teachings of the synagogue or church. By assigning to each feature of a text a hidden, symbolic, or mystical meaning beyond the primary meaning that the words convey in their literal sense, the allegorical interpretation seeks to make the text more comprehensible, acceptable, and relevant to the present.
>
> —*Encyclopaedia Britannica*, 15th Edition

example, gold is good; wood is bad. One will remain, and one will get burned up. But since Paul gave us six possible materials, he clearly intended an expression of increasing or decreasing value.

So Paul's clear intention was to tell us that these "building materials" have certain values in relationship to each other—but still, he did not tell us specifically what these materials represent. Nevertheless, we can assume Paul wanted us to fill in these blanks, so it might be possible to get different answers to the question of what makes a "good Christian."

Did the apostle allow for this anywhere else? Yes, when it comes to the "nonessentials" of the faith, he did indeed. In fact, he tied this concept to the judgment seat of Christ:

> One man considers one day more sacred than another; another man considers every day alike. Each one should be fully convinced in his own mind. He who regards one day as special, does so to the Lord. He who eats meat, eats to the Lord, for he gives thanks to God; and he who abstains, does so to the Lord and gives thanks to God. For none of us lives to himself alone and none of us dies to himself alone. If we live, we live to the Lord; and if we die, we die to the Lord. So, whether we live or die, we belong to the Lord.

> For this very reason, Christ died and returned to life so that he might be the Lord of both the dead and the living. You, then, why do you judge your brother? Or why do you look down on your brother? For we will all stand before God's judgment seat. It is written: "'As surely as I live,' says the Lord, 'every knee will bow before me; every tongue will confess to God.'" So then, each of us will give an account of himself to God. (Rom. 14:5–12)

In this passage, Paul told us that we are all going to stand before Christ to be evaluated. Thus, it is up to us fill in the blanks in such a way that is biblically consistent and that honors God.

Fundamentals versus Nonessentials

Whenever there's a serious snowstorm, my family turns on the TV to see if our school district is on a two-hour delay or closed altogether. We live in a military town, so the bases also have similar delays and closings. However, when they make their announcements, they usually say something like, "All nonessential personnel need not report."

Yikes! I'd hate to have the label "nonessential," no matter how lacking in glory my job could be. But the military makes this designation to indicate what jobs are absolutely necessary to keep the country well defended and what jobs we can temporarily put on hold without compromising national security.

Along the same lines, Christians have long believed that there are certain nonessentials of the faith, certain traditional, more cultural beliefs that, while we may hold them dear, do not impact the integrity of our salvation. This concept of a nonessential doctrine comes from the apostle Paul's admonition in Romans 14:

> Accept him whose faith is weak, without passing judgment on disputable matters. One man's faith allows him to eat everything, but another man, whose faith is weak, eats only vegetables. (vv. 1–2)

The nonessentials described in this passage include dietary restrictions and holidays—namely, beliefs about things that would not threaten anyone's soul if that person were to hold them. In the case of these nonessentials, each man should be "convinced in his own mind" (v. 5). For these beliefs, every man will be judged according to his conviction and how he acted upon those convictions.

God clearly leaves some of these nonessential issues up to the individual. However, once we've made a decision, he wants us to keep the commitment—or not worry about our lack of commitment to a certain way of doing things.

> The man who eats everything must not look down on him who does not, and the man who does not eat everything must not condemn the man who does, for God has accepted him. (v. 3)

My kids' school has a policy against put-downs; any kid caught "dissing" another gets promptly sent to the principal. This would be a great policy for the church; we are not to look down our noses because someone does or does not practice one of the nonessentials:

> Who are you to judge someone else's servant? To his own master he stands or falls. And he will stand, for the Lord is able to make him stand.
> One man considers one day more sacred than another; another man considers every day alike. Each one should be fully convinced in his own mind. (vv. 4–5)

That's the key: being convinced in your own mind.

We need to be careful here, though. The world wants us to have this attitude about *everything*. You know, whatever seems right to you must be true for you. It's all a matter of just being convinced. The scope of Paul's thinking here, though, is clearly defined. This only applies to the nonessentials, in this case, to matters of diet and holiday keeping.

> He who regards one day as special, does so to the Lord. He who eats meat, eats to the Lord, for he gives thanks to God; and he who abstains, does so to the Lord and gives thanks to God. For none of us lives to himself alone and none of us dies to himself alone. If we live, we live to the Lord; and if we die, we die to the Lord. So, whether we live or die, we belong to the Lord. (vv. 6–8)

Let this be the criterion for which we are judged: that in everything we do, we give the Lord preeminence.

> For this very reason, Christ died and returned to life so that he might be the Lord of both the dead and the living. You, then, why do you judge your brother? Or why do you look down on your brother? For we will all stand before God's judgment seat. (vv. 9–10)

By the way, this is the first indication in Paul's writings that Christians will be judged. Of course, he goes into greater detail in 1 Corinthians 3, but he introduces the concept here.

Clearly, when it comes to orthodoxy or moral issues, the church has an obligation to speak up, confront, and draw crystal-clear lines. But in the case of nonessentials, it's better to live and let live and concentrate on that upon which we do agree.

> It is written: "'As surely as I live,' says the Lord, 'every knee will bow before me; every tongue will confess to God.'" So then, each of us will give an account of himself to God. (Rom. 14:11–12)

There it is again. Since God is going to have the final word in all matters, regardless of significance, we have the freedom to just let certain things go, knowing that the Lord is going to have the final word in the matter.

In these nonessential matters, two men with completely opposite beliefs may be rewarded in exactly the same manner because they practiced their beliefs regarding the nonessentials with equal vigor, enthusiasm, and passion.

So what approach can we take that will fit these criteria? The "building materials," biblically speaking, could be many things. We could say that they represent spiritual gifts and how effectively we use them. We could say that they represent the fruit of the Spirit and the degrees to which they manifest themselves in our lives. We could say that they represent spiritual disciplines (prayer, Bible study, serving, fasting, worship, fellowship, confession, etc.).

Paying Peter to Interpret Paul

Since Paul does not define what the materials are, any of these would be legitimate criteria from which to apply 1 Corinthians 3:11–15, because they are all biblically based—and Paul certainly makes mention of these interpretive criteria in his other letters.

In this book, our "interpretive filter" is going to be the list of traits that the apostle Peter used to introduce his second epistle:

> Grace and peace be yours in abundance through the knowledge of God and of Jesus our Lord.
>
> His divine power has given us everything we need for life and godliness through our knowledge of him who called us by his own glory and goodness. Through these he has given us his very great and precious promises, so that through them you may participate in the divine nature and escape the corruption in the world caused by evil desires.
>
> For this very reason, make every effort to add to your faith goodness; and to goodness, knowledge; and to knowledge, self-control; and

WHAT IS BIBLICAL FRUIT?

One of the first commandments in the Scriptures is to bear fruit and multiply (see Gen. 1:28). The first order of business for Mr. and Mrs. Adam? Start making babies. That is clearly the context. But then the commandment expands to talk about their work bearing fruit. God expected their garden to thrive because their hard and creative work would eventually pay off. (Keep in mind, this all happened before the fall).

As is the case in many of the Scriptures, who is actually bearing the fruit seems to switch off between man and God. One of my favorite passages along these lines is in Deuteronomy, where the Lord says,

You may say to yourself, "My power and the strength of my hands have

---

to self-control, perseverance; and to perseverance, godliness; and to godliness, brotherly kindness; and to brotherly kindness, love. For if you possess these qualities in increasing measure, they will keep you from being ineffective and unproductive in your knowledge of our Lord Jesus Christ. But if anyone does not have them, he is nearsighted and blind, and has forgotten that he has been cleansed from his past sins.

Therefore, my brothers, be all the more eager to make your calling and election sure. For if you do these things, you will never fall, and you will receive a rich welcome into the eternal kingdom of our Lord and Savior Jesus Christ. (1:2–11)

It's important to say up front that Peter obviously did not write this passage as a commentary on Paul's teaching in 1 Corinthians 3. Bible scholars are not even sure which of the two passages was written first. But if we move forward with the assumption that the Holy Spirit inspired both passages and that both passages are talking about similar topics, then their teachings are not only going to be consistent, but one can help interpret the produced this wealth for me." But remember the LORD your God, for it is he who gives you the ability to produce wealth, and so confirms his covenant, which he swore to your forefathers, as it is today. (8:17–18)

Biblical fruit includes children, whether they are biological or spiritual (see Mal. 2:15; 1 Cor. 4:17). Biblical fruit includes the rewards of labor, the tangible results of our hard work. And, finally, fruit is a reflection of the work of the Holy Spirit in our lives, namely, the fruit of the Spirit. This is not simply God making us into nice people, but his work of conforming us gradually, day by day, into the image of Christ, with every adventure that he leads us into.

---

other. This is one way that we are able to use Scripture to interpret Scripture.

Even Peter admits that Paul wrote some things that were difficult to understand:

> Bear in mind that our Lord's patience means salvation, just as our dear brother Paul also wrote you with the wisdom that God gave him. He writes the same way in all his letters, speaking in them of these matters. His letters contain some things that are hard to understand, which ignorant and unstable people distort, as they do the other Scriptures, to their own destruction. (2 Peter 3:15–16)

There are many parallels in these passages that lend themselves well to using one biblical author to interpret the other.

1. Both begin with God's grace, apart from which any sort of evaluation is meaningless and trite:

KINGDOM SPOTLIGHT
THE BEST OF ALL POSSIBLE KINGDOMS

The kingdom of God has always existed. Dr. Dallas Willard's definition of the kingdom of God is the "effective range of God's rule."[3] According to this definition then, the kingdom of God has existed for as long as God has existed. That is, it is without beginning, and it shall never end. The kingdom of God existed before the foundation of the world, even before the creation of angels. The kingdom of God existed when only the three persons of the Godhead existed—and even then, God ruled.

Historical Christian teaching asserts that the members of the Trinity—Father, Son, and Spirit—are all equally God. But the Son and the Spirit voluntarily remain in submission to the Father, and they have existed in this state of benevolent hierarchy from all eternity, without even a nanosecond of resistance or disharmony.

Then the kingdom of God "expanded," as it were, with the creation of angels and the dominions over which they ruled. One of those angels was Lucifer, who had been given supreme position above all the other angels, again in a system of benevolent hierarchy. They were given responsibility in these newly created realms as rulers, powers, and authorities.

When God decided to create the world as we know it, the kingdom of God expanded even further. As we will discuss, God created the best of all possible worlds, one in which existed free will—a system wherein God remains totally sovereign and yet each created being remains morally responsible for his or her thoughts, words, and actions.

No one wants to be loved by someone who has been coerced into doing so. So it is with God. As the story goes, Lucifer exercised his free will, cultivated and nurtured the desire to replace God, and was able to win over the hearts of some of his fellow angelic beings. So they fell with him.

So, for the first time in God's dominion, resistance was allowed to exist.

By the grace God has given me, I laid a foundation as an expert builder, and someone else is building on it. But each one should be careful how he builds. (1 Cor. 3:10)

Grace and peace be yours in abundance through the knowledge of God and of Jesus our Lord. (2 Peter 1:2)

2. Both build their teaching upon the foundation of faith in Jesus Christ:

> For no one can lay any foundation other than the one already laid, which is Jesus Christ. (1 Cor. 3:11)

> For this very reason, make every effort to add to your faith. (2 Peter 1:5)

3. Both speak of qualities or traits that are not only spiritually important but also can exist in varying degrees of strength:

> If any man builds on this foundation using gold, silver, costly stones, wood, hay or straw ... (1 Cor. 3:12)

> For if you possess these qualities in increasing measure, they will keep you from being ineffective and unproductive in your knowledge of our Lord Jesus Christ. (2 Peter 1:8)

4. Both address the possibility of mediocrity and loss in the life of the believer:

> If it is burned up, he will suffer loss; he himself will be saved, but only as one escaping through the flames. (1 Cor. 3:15)

> But if anyone does not have them, he is nearsighted and blind, and has forgotten that he has been cleansed from his past sins. (2 Peter 1:9)

5. And, finally, both imply the possibility of rich reward at the judgment seat of Christ:

His work will be shown for what it is, because the Day will bring it to light. It will be revealed with fire, and the fire will test the quality of each man's work. If what he has built survives, he will receive his reward. (1 Cor. 3:13–14)

You will receive a rich welcome into the eternal kingdom of our Lord and Savior Jesus Christ. (2 Peter 1:11)

Again, the prizes, the rich welcome, the jewels in our crowns are all reflections of this central relational truth: God, from whom we can hide *nothing*, will reward us according to how much he trusts us.

Let's begin this discussion about God's trust in the only place we can legitimately start: God's grace.

CHAPTER 4

GRACE:
Jesus' Personal Relationship with the Unsaved

GRACE: 1. Mercy; clemency. 2. A disposition to be generous or helpful; goodwill. 3. A favor rendered by one who need not do so. 4. A temporary immunity or exemption; a reprieve. 5. Divine love and protection bestowed freely on people. 6. The state of being protected or sanctified by the favor of God. 7. An excellence or power granted by God.

Answers.com

When the nineteenth-century Spanish general Ramon Narvaez was on his deathbed, a priest visited him. Eventually the discussion came around to the condition of the officer's soul.

The priest asked, "Sir, have you forgiven your enemies?"

"I have no need to forgive them," the soldier weakly replied. "I've had them all shot."

The myth of the dramatic deathbed conversion is usually just that: a myth. When dying, a person who has spent a lifetime ignoring God is usually still ambivalent about what awaits him beyond death's door.

Consider this quote that was offered two hundred years prior to the Spanish general's death:

Do we think that when the day has been idly spent and squandered away by us, we shall be fit to work when the night and darkness come—when our understanding is weak, and our memory frail, and our will crooked, and by long custom of sinning obstinately bent the wrong way, what can we then do in religion? What reasonable or acceptable service can we then perform to God? When our candle is just sinking into the socket, how shall our light "so shine before men that they may see our good works"? ... I will not pronounce anything concerning the impossibility of a deathbed repentance, but I am sure that it is very difficult, and, I believe, very rare.[1]

But, of course, when it comes to the grace of God, there are always exceptions.

We hear stories all the time of people experiencing the unfathomable mercy of God and finally becoming reconciled to Christ in their sixties, seventies, and beyond. And sometimes this happens after decades of blatant immorality or perhaps even passive indifference to the things that matter to God. As Jesus reminds us, those who have been forgiven much usually end up loving much and become unstoppable for the kingdom (see Luke 7:47).

When it comes to heavenly rewards, Jesus told an interesting parable that seems to indicate that everyone will get the same prize, regardless of when they entered the kingdom. He understood that there would be people looking for him at different stages in life. The parable was about a vineyard owner who needed help with his harvest. While there were very few, if any, organized temp agencies in the first century, it was quite common in Bible times for able-bodied individuals to wait in the village square and offer themselves as field laborers.

For the kingdom of heaven is like a landowner who went out early in the morning to hire men to work in his vineyard. He agreed to pay them a denarius for the day and sent them into his vineyard.

> About the third hour he went out and saw others standing in the marketplace doing nothing. He told them, "You also go and work in my vineyard, and I will pay you whatever is right." So they went.
>
> He went out again about the sixth hour and the ninth hour and did the same thing. About the eleventh hour he went out and found still others standing around. He asked them, "Why have you been standing here all day long doing nothing?"
>
> "Because no one has hired us," they answered.
>
> He said to them, "You also go and work in my vineyard." (Matt. 20:1–7)

In those days, a worker did not have to wait two weeks to get a paycheck. He received his wages at the end of the day. If he was hired for a job, the employer probably fed him during the time he worked. Of course, that was considered part of the compensation.

We see this idea reflected in Paul's second letter to the Thessalonians. What we gather from his letter is that a few were giving up on "working life" because Jesus was soon to return anyway, so why bother? "Forget that," said the apostle (in essence). "If a man will not work, he shall not eat" (3:10).

When a man was hired, he expected his wages as the sun was setting. He wanted to be able to eat that night, especially since he did not know whether he would have a job the following morning.

> When evening came, the owner of the vineyard said to his foreman, "Call the workers and pay them their wages, beginning with the last ones hired and going on to the first."
>
> The workers who were hired about the eleventh hour came and each received a denarius. (Matt. 20:8–9)

These particular end-of-the-day workers seemed to be getting an exceptional deal. There were certainly ways to break up a denarius (shekels, bushels of grain, etc.). Since a few had really worked only an hour, they were undoubtedly surprised by, and probably grateful for, the vineyard owner's generosity.

This was not true, however, of those men who had been hired earlier in the day. When they realized that they would get no more than the one-hour workers, they were very disappointed and probably just a little miffed.

But the vineyard owner gave them only what they had agreed to. The owner made it clear that he wasn't gypping anyone. He did, however, have the right to be generous, so he decided to exercise that privilege. As far as he was concerned, they were even. He had done everything he had agreed to do.

In this parable, the reward doesn't seem to be commensurate with the service. If the vineyard owner represents God (which seems to be the case), then his generosity must be representative of God's grace. People experience the saving grace of God at different stages in life, and the gift of salvation is the same for all—no matter when they turn to God.

Statistics tell us that most Christians were reconciled with God sometime in their teens, when they "crossed the bridge" from believing because their parents believed to actually owning their faith. Obviously, some people miss this window and either never internalize their faith (usually a passive mistake) or simply reject God altogether. And God, in his grace, still pursues and rescues some of them.

What seems odd about this story is the apparent jealousy of the "veteran believers." Why would a Christian be disappointed that someone else has been blessed by God? This common problem reminds us of the older brother in the story of the prodigal son. When the reckless younger brother returned home, seeking and receiving mercy, the older brother went into his room to pout. *No party for me after all these faithful years of service? Hmmmph.* The father reassured the older brother of his love and gratitude. But there was something else there that was worth celebrating, so it was time for the older brother to grow up and join the party.

The hard truth of this lesson is this: Sometimes we are disappointed when God blesses people in different ways than he has blessed us. And if we're honest, we'll admit that sometimes that makes us feel a little ripped off. We hear testimonies of people who spent their lives doing drugs, cheating people, committing all sorts of crimes, only to be restored by God's grace. They go on to tell their stories in national magazines and in front of thousands of people on TV. In contrast, most of us have spent our lives keeping our noses clean and doing things for God that don't seem to get much notice.

When others are being blessed in areas of life that we seem to be missing out on, let's keep the following things in mind:

1. God is going to keep his agreement with us, even though others appear to be blessed in ways that seem to have eluded us. Keep a daily journal of God's blessings in your life, and review the entries before you go to bed each night. You might be surprised to see the ways you forget how actively God is involved in your life. He's going to keep caring about you, providing for you, and making you more like Jesus, just like he promised to do.

2. Just because God blesses someone doesn't mean he loves the rest of us any less. For those of us who have children, grandchildren, nieces, and nephews, we know the pressure there is to treat all of them fairly. Sometimes special treatment results in the poutiness of the ones who feel cheated. The same dynamic is here when we see God blessing others. The difficult thing to do in these cases is to put away any childish attitudes and rejoice with those who rejoice.

3. Keep in mind that this seems to be the only parable of this sort where everyone's getting the same reward. Other parables and Scriptures make it clear that each person will be rewarded according to what he or she has done. So there's nothing in God's

biblical compensation plan to suggest that everyone gets the same prize. There are clearly degrees of reward in heaven, and God is never going to be unjust in the ways that those rewards are distributed.

So in regard to heavenly rewards, this is the lesson of the parable: When it comes to salvation, the grace of God is no respecter of persons. It's offered and available to all, and it's the same reward for everyone, no matter in what stage of life it's accepted.

Jesus Has a Personal Relationship with the Unsaved

It's common to say that Christians, once they believed, entered into a personal relationship with God. I've got news for you: Their personal relationships with God began long, long before they were saved. That relationship may have been hostile, adversarial, one sided, and supremely frustrating; but it was a relationship all the same.

> [God] is kind to the ungrateful and wicked. (Luke 6:35)

Let's look at some biblical examples of God's grace as shown in his relational pursuit of people who wanted very little to do with him. Consider God's relationship with the world's first murderer.

Cain: Mercy for the Merciless

Cain, as well as his brother Abel, was born after the fall. Both clearly had sinful natures inherited from their parents, but they were going down different spiritual paths. The first symbolic sacrifice for sin probably happened when God killed some sort of animal to clothe the shamed Adam and Eve. The Bible is not clear about how sacrifices evolved from that first event, but it was apparent that Abel understood their significance and that Cain clearly did not. Cain offered fruits and grains, and Abel offered something from his livestock (see Gen. 4:3–5).

By faith Abel offered God a better sacrifice than Cain did. By faith he was commended as a righteous man, when God spoke well of his offerings. And by faith he still speaks, even though he is dead. (Heb. 11:4)

We see later in the Old Testament that both of these sacrifices were acceptable for different purposes, so it was not the substance of the sacrifice that God either accepted or rejected, but the attitude of the one who offered it. Knowing what was in each of the men's respective hearts, God accepted Abel's sacrifice but rejected Cain's.

Then the Lord said to Cain, "Why are you angry? Why is your face downcast?" (Gen. 4:6)

Genuinely concerned for the man's welfare, God inquires as to why Cain felt the way he did. Of course, God knew exactly why Cain was pouting. So why did God even bother asking if he already knew? He clearly wanted Cain to articulate his feelings, to speak for himself. God understands the benefit of defining how we feel so that we can adequately deal with the problem causing those feelings.

But the Bible records no answer from Cain. As we see later in this passage, God warned Cain about "sin crouching at the door" (see Gen. 4:7), which was presumably Cain's inability to control his resentment. But apparently God's concern did not prevent Cain from allowing his disappointment to turn to envy and then eventually to homicidal rage.

Cain's response to God's admonition was to deceive his sibling by luring him out to a field, where the chance of discovery was diminished, and there he killed his younger brother.

Then the Lord said to Cain, "Where is your brother Abel?" "I don't know," he replied. "Am I my brother's keeper?" (Gen. 4:9)

Again, God knew exactly where Abel was. Abel's soul was probably standing right next to him when the Lord asked the question. Again, God was giving Cain a chance to speak for himself, to articulate what he felt. Perhaps God was also giving Cain a chance to confess his sin and lack of faith.

Cain refused the invitation and smugly replied that he was not his little brother's babysitter. Obviously, Cain had no real idea of the power of God, nor his omniscience. Perhaps Cain thought that since he was in a field and apparently unnoticed, his murderous deed would remain undiscovered.

Cain couldn't have been more wrong. God condemned Cain for spilling his brother's blood and sentenced him to a lifetime of wandering. Apparently, Cain interpreted this as God's abandonment of him, and he panicked.

> Cain said to the Lord, "My punishment is more than I can bear." (Gen. 4:13)

Consider this: The man who refused to show mercy was now asking for mercy. And amazingly enough, God granted it. God, in his grace, offered mercy to the man who had denied it to his brother. God is kind even to those who are evil and self-absorbed.

In another place in the Bible we are told that it is the kindness of God that leads some people to repentance (Rom. 2:4). Perhaps that was the Lord's motivation here: He wanted Cain to repent, to acknowledge that his problem was his rage, not God, not his brother, not even his parents, who had lost their home.

One has to wonder if Cain ever wandered back to the entrance of the garden of Eden to see the flaming sword that prevented him and his family from ever going back in. Knowing Cain, it probably provoked even more resentment in him. Perhaps that was Cain's sin and the reason God rejected his sacrifice.

Balaam: The Man Who Talked with His Donkey

Balaam was another feisty character with whom the Lord had a very contentious relationship. Balaam was more or less a prophet for hire. For the right price he would bless or curse whomever you wished. But the man knew his limits; he understood the length of the Lord's leash when it came to his corruption.

Balak, the king of Moab, was getting a little worried about the increasing number of Israelites in his backyard. He had seen what they had done to the Amorites, and he probably figured it was only a matter of time before they set their sights on his land. So Balak sought out Balaam, the spiritual hit man, to come and curse the people of God so the king and his princes could have a measure of security.

> God came to Balaam and asked, "Who are these men with you?" (Num. 22:9)

Once again, God was asking a question to which he already knew the answer. This was not to mock Balaam, but to get him to articulate the problems he was about to create for himself. Balak was depending on sorcery and divination to take care of his problems, and the Lord was going to make sure (at least in this case) that his name was not going to be associated with any sort of spell casting.

God allowed Balaam to go but made it crystal clear where Balaam's greed ended and God's will began. To make sure there was no miscommunication between them, he sent an angel with a flaming sword to further confront the prophet. If it hadn't been for Balaam's stubborn donkey, Balaam may have never had his first conversation with Balak. What's really amazing about this story is not that the donkey talked, but that Balaam had a conversation with the animal.

Despite Balak's best efforts, Balaam ended up blessing instead of cursing Israel. In fact, he gave multiple blessings. Even so, Balaam found a way around God's guidelines for blessing and found a different way to get Balak what he wanted:

> Nevertheless, I have a few things against you: You have people there who hold to the teaching of Balaam, who taught Balak to entice the Israelites to sin by eating food sacrificed to idols and by committing sexual immorality. (Rev. 2:14)

Even Jesus himself condemned Balaam as one who set the pattern of the abuse of religious power and authority by enticing people to do things clearly contrary to the will of God.

After Balaam's blessings, we don't hear again from the pseudo-prophet. But the accounts following Balaam's story about Israel's sudden lapse into idolatry and sexual immorality can apparently be attributed to him. Sometime later, Israel's army killed Balaam.

God's relationships with both Cain and Balaam were marked by confrontation, hostility, contempt, and indifference. New Testament references to these two men seem to indicate that they were never reconciled with God.

> Do not be like Cain, who belonged to the evil one and murdered his brother. And why did he murder him? Because his own actions were evil and his brother's were righteous. (1 John 3:12)

> They have left the straight way and wandered off to follow the way of Balaam son of Beor, who loved the wages of wickedness. (2 Peter 2:15)

> Woe to them [men who speak abusively about what they do not understand]! They have taken the way of Cain; they have rushed for profit into Balaam's error. (Jude v. 11)

KINGDOM SPOTLIGHT
HEAVENLY REBELLION, EARTHLY FUTILITY

Good people are often naive about evil. They simply cannot fathom a human (or angelic) heart that is entirely free of conscience or the ability to empathize. In the case of angelic beings, we must realize that those who fell are utterly and decisively beyond redemption. Why this is true for the angels and not for human beings is one of those "secrets of God" that he has not deemed fit to reveal.

Perhaps it has something to do with angels not being created in the image of God. When they decided to place their bets on Lucifer (who, no doubt, promised them immunity from God's judgment), it became an eternal watershed moment for them. They made a decision they could never retract. (In fact, they would never have any desire to do so, even when they faced their inevitable damnation.)

Can angels still fall? The biblical record is silent on this, so it would be presumptuous to speculate. However, most Christians believe that once the angels had chosen between God and Satan, they had made an eternal decision.

Those who did fall now make up the supernatural energizing forces behind the human resistance to the kingdom of God.

Like the fallen angels, each rebellious human being is committed to creating and setting up his own minikingdom. As sinful people, we often mistake being made in the image of God with being God, so we try to create our own little universes with each of us at the center of them.

If we were only able to catch a glimpse of this from God's perspective, we would see how utterly silly this looks—like a little biosphere bobbling in a vast ocean, thinking that it *is* the entire ocean—when, of course, nothing could be further from the truth.

What can we learn about grace from God's relationships with Cain and Balaam? We learn that God will not stop pursuing someone as long as that person is capable of responding to him. The presence of God's grace does not mean that problems will be ignored; in fact, God in his mercy will push the wayward to clearly define their problems so they can be decisively confronted. God was able to demonstrate compassion without diminishing the horrific

HEROD: A WILY FOX

No doubt about it: Jesus and the Herods were enemies.

The first Herod ordered the slaughter of all the male babies after Jesus was born. Certainly, this created an enormous burden of grief (not guilt, of course) that Jesus carried throughout his life. Herod II had John the Baptist beheaded, killing Jesus' messenger. And then, at the end of Jesus' life, the same Herod mockingly demanded a miracle of the Christ.

While Jesus and Herod II did not speak face-to-face until the very end of Jesus' life, the Lord did convey a message to Herod. Jesus gave him the unflattering moniker of "fox" to highlight the man's deceptive nature, one

---

deeds of either Cain or Balaam. And God clearly did everything he could to be reconciled with both of them, but ultimately, they refused.

Among other grace stories in the Old Testament, at least two had apparently happier endings: the stories of God's respective relationships with Hagar and Naaman.

Hagar: Maid, Mistress, and Mother

Hagar was a handful. Apparently she wasn't too politically savvy when it came to dealing with her employer, Sarah. Of course, Sarah's suggestion that Abraham have her baby via Hagar wasn't too bright either. But Sarah was the one with the authority, and the overconfident Hagar suddenly found herself on the wrong side of the power play and was pushed out into an unforgiving wilderness with her baby.

> The angel of the LORD found Hagar near a spring in the desert; it was the spring that is beside the road to Shur. And he said, "Hagar, servant of Sarai, where have you come from, and where are you going?"
>
> "I'm running away from my mistress Sarai," she answered. (Gen. 16:7–8)

that he clearly inherited from his ancestor. Then Jesus left him with an enigmatic riddle:

> At that time some Pharisees came to Jesus and said to him, "Leave this place and go somewhere else. Herod wants to kill you."
> He replied, "Go tell that fox, 'I will drive out demons and heal people today and tomorrow, and on the third day I will reach my goal.'" (Luke 13:31–32)
>
> Jesus made clear to this narcissistic ruler that it was the Son of God, not Herod, who would determine the time of Jesus' death.

Again, as with Cain, we see God asking Hagar to define her problem. Instead of defiance, however, Hagar explained her problem and then accepted the Lord's instruction to return to Abraham and Sarah—where she was apparently taken back. Later when Hagar was cast out for good, the Lord continued to protect her, provide for her, and allow the descendants of her son Ishmael to thrive.

Of course, Ishmael's descendants later became some of Israel's fiercest enemies and remained so for thousands of years, generation after generation, even to this very day.

What can we learn from this? Abraham and Sarah agreed to try to hasten the promise of God, resulting in centuries of abuse and strife for God's people. Adam and Eve agreed to doubt God's integrity and introduced sin into the world. Ananias and Sapphira agreed to lie to church leaders, and both were carried out of the church without a pulse. All this is to say that if you're married, be careful that any agreements you make are clearly within the will of God, because the consequences may be significant, and the ripple effect may go on for generations. Of course, the same is true for those spousal agreements that do honor God. Consider the ministry of Aquila and Priscilla; they seemed to work very well together, especially when it came to ministering to Apollos and Paul.

Hagar had a problem with sarcasm and mockery. She disdained the very people who were sustaining her. But even when she suffered the consequences of her foolish behavior, God's grace was there for her. And she responded with gratitude:

> [Hagar] gave this name to the LORD who spoke to her: "You are the God who sees me," for she said, "I have now seen the One who sees me." (Gen. 16:13)

Another proud individual in the Old Testament was Naaman.

Namaan: Leader and Leper

> Naaman was commander of the army of the king of Aram. He was a great man in the sight of his master and highly regarded, because through him the LORD had given victory to Aram. He was a valiant soldier, but he had leprosy. (2 Kings 5:1)

While Naaman did not have to worry about being exiled because of his leprosy, he did have to worry about dying. During Bible times, leprosy was a devastating disease that killed the body's ability to feel pain. While some might consider this a blessing, it is physical pain that usually tells us a problem exists and needs to be addressed. Most of the people who suffered from this contagious illness usually died of infections caused by undetected wounds. Surely Naaman had seen what had happened to those who contracted this disease, so he sought supernatural help.

> So Naaman went with his horses and chariots and stopped at the door of Elisha's house. Elisha sent a messenger to say to him, "Go, wash yourself seven times in the Jordan, and your flesh will be restored and you will be cleansed." (2 Kings 5:9–10)

Surprisingly, these instructions angered Naaman. He expected Elisha to simply wave his hand to take care of the problem. Some astute servants, however, talked him into following the prophet's instructions. When he followed those instructions, he was healed.

Despite the man's arrogance, God showed him grace and removed a very serious problem from his life. Like Hagar, Naaman was humbled and expressed his reverence and gratitude to God:

> Naaman and all his attendants went back to the man of God. He stood before him and said, "Now I know that there is no God in all the world except in Israel." (2 Kings 5:15)

Even when Naaman asked to be excused and forgiven for bowing down in a pagan temple (for political reasons), God was gracious and sent him off in peace.

Jesus referred to Naaman in Luke 4. He pointed out that Naaman was a Gentile who was healed while many in Israel were not (see v. 27). This angered many of the religious leaders who heard Jesus' words, because his statement exposed their false belief that somehow God favored them above all other groups, no matter how corrupt they became.

Others Who Experienced Grace

We could site example after example of God's grace in the Bible. After civil war resulted in the division of Israel and Judah, both sides had many evil kings. Through the prophets, the Lord continuously chided them for their wrongdoing and lack of compassion.

And yet, when they humbled themselves, God was there, ready to be reconciled with them, pulling back on his intended discipline, ready yet again to give them another chance.

This was certainly true of Ahab, the ferocious but horribly insecure king of Israel who caused nothing but trouble for God's people, and most notably for Elijah.

But when Ahab humbled himself, God relented from his judgment:

> Have you noticed how Ahab has humbled himself before me? Because he has humbled himself, I will not bring this disaster in his day, but I will bring it on his house in the days of his son. (1 Kings 21:29)

The same happened with Rehoboam, the arrogant son of Solomon who took the advice of his young friend over that of his father's seasoned counselors. God showed him mercy at the first sign of genuine humility:

> Because Rehoboam humbled himself, the LORD's anger turned from him, and he was not totally destroyed. (2 Chron. 12:12)

Manasseh, probably one of the most corrupt of all the kings in Israel or Judah, was also shown mercy when he demonstrated humility. This man placed his own screaming babies in the fiery belly of the idol Molech in hope of a better harvest from this pretend god. And even Manasseh was shown mercy and acknowledged God's sovereignty when things got bad enough:

> In his [Manasseh's] distress he sought the favor of the LORD his God and humbled himself greatly before the God of his fathers. And when he prayed to him, the LORD was moved by his entreaty and listened to his plea; so he brought him back to Jerusalem and to his kingdom. Then Manasseh knew that the LORD is God. (2 Chron. 33:12–13)

GRACE

So what can we learn about grace from these Old Testament characters?

First, we must acknowledge that, in some ways, we are no different from any of them. Every Christian has on his spiritual résumé the job title "Former Enemy of God."

> All of us also lived among them at one time, gratifying the cravings of our sinful nature and following its desires and thoughts. Like the rest, we were by nature objects of wrath. (Eph. 2:3)

> At one time we too were foolish, disobedient, deceived and enslaved by all kinds of passions and pleasures. We lived in malice and envy, being hated and hating one another. (Titus 3:3)

> Do you not know that the wicked will not inherit the kingdom of God? Do not be deceived: Neither the sexually immoral nor idolaters nor adulterers nor male prostitutes nor homosexual offenders nor thieves nor the greedy nor drunkards nor slanderers nor swindlers will inherit the kingdom of God. *And that is what some of you were.* But you were washed, you were sanctified, you were justified in the name of the Lord Jesus Christ and by the Spirit of our God. (1 Cor. 6:9–11)

Peter and Paul made it clear that any discussion about earthly or heavenly rewards must first start with grace. Apart from grace, there would be no dominion in which to serve God. Everything that follows is meaningless apart from grace, so grace must become our starting point.

Only when we have grasped the immeasurable patience and compassion of God's mercy can we even begin to understand saving faith, which we must experience before God can even begin to trust us. Do you understand that God initiates any relationship with him? He is supremely interested in being reconciled with us. Usually when there's a rift in a relationship, both parties involved have contributed to the problem. Not so in any relationship with

God. We are the problem. Period. God, in his grace, initiates, pursues, and provides a solution.

The person whom God trusts understands that any discussion of personal reward must begin with God's grace. He alone initiates and sustains our ability to do *anything*, either within or outside of his dominion.

Not Far from the Kingdom

> When Jesus saw that he had answered wisely, he said to him, "You are not far from the kingdom of God." And from then on no one dared ask him any more questions. (Mark 12:34)

One of the most intriguing encounters Jesus had was with a teacher of the law. It was a friendly encounter, which seems a bit out of place for the context. Jesus had just cleared the temple, had been confronted by the chief priests about his authority, and then had delivered one of his zinger parables to expose the greed and hypocrisy of the religious leaders in Jerusalem. Then they sent some Pharisees and Herodians over to Jesus to see if they could trap him into saying something inflammatory. They failed. Then the Sadducees took at stab at pushing Jesus into a theological corner, but he easily turned them on their heads.

In the middle of all of these hostile encounters, Jesus fielded another question, this time from one of the teachers of the law. Since the religious leaders had been sending out all of their heavy hitters, Jesus might have expected this to be another attempted trap. But being fully God and knowing their thoughts, Jesus understood the man's sincerity and answered his question: "Of all the commandments, which is the most important?" (Mark 12:28). Jesus replied, "Love God will all your heart, mind, and soul. And love your neighbor as yourself" (see v. 30).

Then this teacher of the law essentially paraphrased Jesus' answer, demonstrating that he not only understood Jesus but also agreed with him! (Keep in mind that this man may have been sent to corner Jesus.)

When Jesus saw that the man had answered wisely, he said an interesting thing: "You are not far from the kingdom of God" (v. 34).

In a crowd of hundreds of hostile people who were probably galaxies away from the kingdom of God, Jesus was able to put a finger on the proximity of this man's potential for being reconciled with God and entering the kingdom.

Many people who cross our paths are also "not far from the kingdom." Don't let outer appearances fool you. They can be exceptionally quiet or downright hostile to anything having to do with God. C. S. Lewis said that when he entered the kingdom, he came in kicking and screaming.[2] You just never know how close someone may be.

Throughout this book, you will be introduced to eight fictional characters who are also "not far from the kingdom." They are seven students and one teacher in a community college course called Two Worldviews. During their discussions, they'll be talking about different worldviews that are in conflict. As we listen in, we will also get an idea of how people who "are not far from the kingdom" think about the plethora of opinions that seems to be out there about life, love, and the meaning of our existence.

Two of these people, in due time, will get married to each other. One becomes homeless but gets back on his feet. Each of these characters, except one, eventually enters the kingdom of God. But you won't read about those things in this book. Their continued adventures will periodically be updated at www.dougschmidt.com and perhaps even fleshed out in a future series.

As you listen, I want you to see how God loves, respects, and protects these folks, even though they have not yet acknowledged their need to be reconciled with him. One of the underlying biblical truths of this book is that Jesus has an ongoing, personal relationship with the unsaved. It may be adversarial and estranged, but it's a relationship nonetheless.

Unknown to the classmates, they have been handpicked by their teacher; they are ordinary but motivated folks who are just taking a night class for a variety of reasons. In their fictional world, some of them will be reading this book along with you. One of their assignments will be to question the author, and you'll be able to read some of their responses.

They are here to give us insight into how some people think—especially those who are on the brink of committing their lives to God. Who knows? You might see yourself in one of their seats.

The Class, First Night

"Good evening. My name is Jacob Prevedel, and you are in a class called Two Worldviews. If you're in the wrong place, this would be the time to slip out."

A few of the students shuffled a bit in their chairs, but nobody got up to leave.

"Great! Well, I've been teaching this course for about six years now, and I love it because the material almost always provokes a lot of discussion. And *that's* what you'll be graded on: your contribution to our ongoing group conversation."

The teacher could tell by his students' faces that his remark about how they would be graded wasn't going to bother any of them. In fact, he knew it wasn't going to be a problem. He had handpicked each one of these students. Every semester, forty to fifty people signed up for this course (a fact that Jake was very proud of), but there was room for only seven. Official school policy stated that when a class was overbooked, there had to be a lottery. But Jake always first showed the list to other teachers and asked them to point out the "talkers." Once Jake had his seven names, he did his own "lottery." The dean knew exactly what he was doing but always looked the other way.

"Since this is a discussion-intense course, we can have our classes in any number of settings: here, the cafeteria, the coffeehouse, the bookstore, the cinema diner. That's the good thing about talking; you can do it just about anywhere."

The students' smiles grew a little.

"The course is called Two Worldviews because we're going to discuss two opposing perspectives every class session. Usually, I'll give you a couple of quotes whose origins come from different parts of the social, political, or religious spectra."

Politics and religion? Sonia thought. *Those discussions don't usually go very well. I'm not sure I wanna do this.*

"My goal in these discussions is not to change your minds. In fact, I'm going to do my best not to tilt my hand in either direction. I may even disagree with both worldviews being presented. However, it is my goal to *sharpen* your minds. At the end of our eight weeks together, I'm hoping that each of you will feel secure enough in your own worldviews to be able to engage with any opposing perspective without feeling threatened or like somehow you're going to lose your identities. That's probably the number one reason why people stay in their rabbit holes: They're afraid they're going to disappear or something if they talk with someone who disagrees with them."

"Hey, Prof, can we bring in our own quotes? Y'know, choose the worldviews we want to systematically dismantle?" Kevin wanted at least one discussion on unacceptable levels of government intrusion.

"Sure, and the best way to do that is to tie it into whatever that week's topic is going to be. If you'll take a look at the syllabus, you will see what the discussion starters are going to be. The class is called Two Worldviews, but two is simply a place to begin. We have to stay on that week's general topic, and it will be my responsibility to keep the conversations in those particular realms. But within those general guidelines, I'll be expecting you to introduce some new materials.

"And, by the way, just call me Jake."

"Don't be afraid, either, to play Devil's advocate for a worldview that may not be your own. It's amazing what you'll learn about yourself by sitting in a 'different chair.' In fact, I don't really want to know where you stand on any particular issue for the first few weeks. So have some fun and play a different part."

I suppose that's safe. Patricia was wondering how Ryan was doing with his new babysitter. *He'll be fine.*

"Now, I schedule this class in the evenings, because, like most of you, I have a day job that I don't intend on quitting any time soon. So, of course, I'm going to respect your time, and I'll assume you'll respect each others'.

"The school requires you to be here for at least three hours for each class session. As soon as we reach that point each class, you're free to go. However, in the past some discussions have gotten rather heated and gone longer. A couple of years ago, we finally stopped when the sun came up. That was a record."

Jacob noticed a few jaws dropping.

I may be chatty, thought Cathy, *but I'm not sticking around for one of those marathons.*

"OK then. We all understand the ground rules?"

Heads nodded.

"All right, let's start with introductions."

Chapter 5

Faith:
Belief and Repentance—A Two-Sided Coin

FAITH: 1. Confident belief in the truth, value, or trustworthiness of a person, idea, or thing. 2. Belief that does not rest on logical proof or material evidence. See synonyms at *belief*. See synonyms at *trust*. 3. Loyalty to a person or thing; allegiance. 4. A set of principles or beliefs. 5. The theological virtue defined as secure belief in God and a trusting acceptance of God's will.

The Free Dictionary

God cannot begin to trust anyone with whom he has not been reconciled.

For this reason, Peter and Paul begin the human element of their teachings (see 1 Cor. 3:2; 2 Peter 1) with faith. (As we've seen, everything ultimately begins with and is sustained by the divine element of grace.)

As we've seen in the previous example, God has an ongoing, dynamic relationship with the unsaved. It's hostile, frustrating, one sided, and characterized by different degrees of estrangement; but it's a relationship nonetheless. God is supremely concerned with getting that relationship "back on track." And that always begins with saving faith. To better understand the nature of saving faith, we should examine those who willfully have none.

When I transferred to a Christian liberal arts college, one of my first classes was called The Nature of Christian Thought. Ironically, it seemed like all we studied was absurdist existentialism (like the movies of Ingmar Bergman and authors like Camus and Sartre). This form of existentialism is called by its proponents "absurd" because it views all of existence as a cruel joke that needs to be overcome. This can never be accomplished, of course, because the cessation of existence always wins. And nonexistence in their worldview is the greatest of all evils.

What this class did for me, however, was to provide a velvety dark background against which to study the diamonds of genuine faith. Taken to its logical conclusion, life without faith, without God, is absolutely and utterly meaningless. And at least the absurdist existentialists are honest enough to admit that.

Of course, they could have saved themselves a lot of trouble by internalizing the "dark side" of the book of Ecclesiastes, because Solomon would have told them exactly the same thing. According to Leland Ryken, the key to understanding the "life is meaningless" sections in Ecclesiastes is to look for the phrase "under the sun." When you read those, look out, because Solomon is about to descend into the abyss of "all is vanity." However, the book of Ecclesiastes is ultimately life affirming, because the biblical author concludes that life is meaningful when it is devoted to obeying God, who clearly does exist.[1]

As we take a look at those who willfully refuse to be reconciled with God, as we mentioned, it's important to distinguish between the human and (fallen) angelic forms of this "disbelief." While they are similar in that they both resist any advancement of God's dominion (and your involvement in it), they are qualitatively different.

The distinction between these human and angelic systems of disbelief is this: The supernatural forces of darkness are fully, utterly, and unalterably beyond redemption. Most have been in the presence of God (with some still appearing before him regularly), and yet they still irredeemably choose to oppose him. Their destructive roles are active and aggressive, and they perform with the full and complete knowledge of what they are doing. And even among them there are degrees of wickedness (see Matt 12:45; Luke 11:26). Some are so bad that God won't even let them out of their dungeons until the time of judgment has come:

> God did not spare angels when they sinned, but sent them to hell, putting them into gloomy dungeons to be held for judgment. (2 Peter 2:4)

This is probably why the demons in the Gerasenes man begged Jesus not to cast them into the Abyss—they knew that once they were there, the little freedom that they had would be gone forever (see Matt. 8:29; Luke 8:31).

The only exception to this seems to be Satan, who is bound and thrown in the Abyss but is allowed to return for a short while. Of course, where you place this event in human history depends upon your eschatology. But boy, if you think he was angry before he was tossed in, you can only imagine the rage he will bring into the world when he receives this short break! In his mind, the release will be of his own doing, and he will believe that it's permanent. Like many of those who follow him, Satan just doesn't get it, and he never will.

A passage in Isaiah is often quoted to help us understand Satan's thinking as he descended into the depths of his irrevocable choice:

> You said in your heart, "I will ascend to heaven; I will raise my throne above the stars of God; I will sit enthroned on the mount of assembly, on the utmost heights of the sacred mountain. I will ascend above the tops of the clouds; I will make myself like the Most High." (14:13–14)

Many have assumed that since the Devil knows that his time is short, he somehow simply resigned to his fate of being cast ultimately into the lake of fire.

> Therefore rejoice, you heavens and you who dwell in them! But woe to the earth and the sea, because the devil has gone down to you! He is filled with fury, because he knows that his time is short. (Rev. 12:12)

Nothing could be further from the truth.

Since Satan believes that his time is short, he is all the more frenetic and enraged about the urgency of his task. Satan and, to different degrees, those angels who followed him are best described as pathological psychopaths who really believe that they can topple God.

The Devil's top priority and supreme goal is to grieve the heart of God. To understand his evil motives, it's helpful to think in terms of a photo negative: Whatever God has defined as good, Satan genuinely believes is evil, and vice versa. It is God's suffering, caused by Satan (and human beings who imitate his way), that gives the Devil sporadic moments of twisted euphoria and false security. These moments seem to suffice to keep him driving toward his utterly insane goal of wresting power from God.

Again, he really believes that he's going to be able to pull this off. There is no hope of reasoning, redemption, or reconciliation with him—or the demonic powers that follow him.

In trying to understand the human element of the powers of darkness, it would be helpful to see the parallels that Jesus made:

> You belong to your father, the devil, and you want to carry out your father's desire. He was a murderer from the beginning, not holding to the truth, for there is no truth in him. When he lies, he speaks his native language, for he is a liar and the father of lies. (John 8:44)

While the human elements that oppose the kingdom of God share a similar mind-set, we must not forget to keep in mind that those who are under the grip of these powers, by their own conscious or passive decision, are clearly *not* beyond redemption. And if they are won over, they become utterly unstoppable in their desire to honor the God who forgave them.

While it might be argued that God, in his sovereignty, knows who will ultimately refuse his grace, there is no indication in the Scriptures that any human being has the ability to discern a person's capacity to be redeemed. Of course, that includes you and me. For this reason, we must never give up on any human being, no matter how wicked and reprobate.

BELIEF

One interesting comparison of human and demonic "belief" is found in the book of James:

> You believe that there is one God. Good! Even the demons believe that—and shudder. (2:19)

James was making two significant points: (1) belief in the existence of God is good, but (2) it's not enough to save you. However, the cognitive side of faith begins with an acknowledgment in the existence of God:

> Without faith it is impossible to please God, because anyone who comes to him must believe that he exists and that he rewards those who earnestly seek him. (Heb. 11:6)

This belief is assumed in most, if not all, of the Scriptures. Many biblical writers assumed that their readers would acknowledge that there is a God is the heavens, even though they might not acknowledge his sovereignty. But today, culturally speaking, we cannot always start with the assumption that people believe in the existence of a personal God. They may believe in a force, a higher power, or their own deity, but not in the personal God of the Bible.

We must not express exasperation over our worldly friends' unwillingness to see the obvious, but rather simply see it as a starting point. C. S. Lewis considered his "primary conversion" to be from atheism to theism. The struggle of the next step of reconciling faith with God seemed relatively minor to him.[2]

In recent days, a British philosopher named Antony Flew has been considered the most significant academic force behind contemporary atheism. And because of the compelling arguments behind the theory of intelligent design, he has now confessed to the logical need for a "unmoved mover" (namely, a supreme being) to be the cause and creative force behind the universe as we see it today.[3] At best, he is now described as a deist, one who believes that God exists but then stepped away from the creation process entirely. Time will tell if Dr. Flew will progress any further in his recently formed theistic beliefs.

Ironically, a few people who deny the existence of God at times will claim to feel close to him. How can you feel close to someone

> *Ideas can be potent, and, sure, they can be "dangerous," but that is all the more reason for Christians not to be afraid of them, but to understand them. For if we don't study the great minds who shaped our world, we'll fail to understand how the people around us today think. Their worldviews will be incomprehensible to us, and we'll have little to offer to challenge those worldviews.*
>
> —CHUCK COLSON, BREAKPOINT

you do not believe exists? In the case of God, many people simply cannot deny his presence in their lives, even though they vehemently oppose any arguments pointing to God's existence.

Are they going to contradict themselves? Of course they are. That's what "being lost" means. When you're walking around in spiritual darkness, you're going to head in several different directions, thinking the whole time that you're heading "due north." In cases like these, it's best to ask the individuals questions about their beliefs that move them toward the logical conclusions of those worldviews. Instead of pointing out the blatantly obvious errors in their thinking, help them to discover them on their own.

So even though we cannot make the assumption of theistic belief (as we could two or three decades ago), there is still hope. The historic pendulum swings back and forth (between "open" and "closed") when it comes to belief in the existence of God. But so what? It does not matter where the pendulum is. What matters is that we're meeting people where they happen to be in the motion of the swinging cultural arm.

This is cognitive faith: to believe in the existence of God. It may even be expanded into the belief that Jesus exists as the Son of God and sits at the right hand of God and makes many claims upon our lives because of his position of trust. The belief aspect of faith is that Jesus Christ is God's son and that he is able and willing to save us.

While there are clearly degrees of intimacy with or estrangement from God, there are only two kinds of relationships with him. You are either an enemy of God, or you have been reconciled with him.

And there are two responses to this fact: (1) You can continue in the false belief that you haven't done anything that would cause your relationship with God to be adversarial or antagonistic, or (2) you can simply acknowledge the fact that you (and not God) are the problem. In response, you may attempt to bear the burden of the damage that has caused your relationship, and you might try to do everything humanly possible to correct the problem. Then ultimately finding that there isn't anything you can do to relieve the strain, you appeal to God for mercy.

This was the prayer of the tax collector, which Jesus said justified the man in his Father's eyes: "God, have mercy on me, a sinner" (Luke 18:13).

We see this humble attitude in Peter when he realized the Lord's holiness and power and his own contrasting condition: "Go away from me, Lord; I am a sinful man!" (Luke 5:8).

Saving faith is reconciling faith, which is described best as two sides of the same coin: One side represents belief, and other side represents repentance. As it flips through the air, it's often difficult to see which is which.

This is the type faith that results in spiritual growth: belief, repentance, appealing to God for mercy, receiving his grace, and moving forward in our walk with him.

This is the person whom God trusts: the one with whom he has been reconciled by faith.

THE CLASS, PART 2

"Ron, why don't we start with you? And if you don't mind, let's go a little beyond name, rank, and serial number. Perhaps you can finish a sentence like, 'I'm really passionate about …' or 'Very few people know this about me' or 'This particular thing, person, event, idea, or issue is very important to me.'"

"Well, my name is Ron Wilhoit, and about four years ago I lost my job and then was offered it back in three months. That's the short version. Little longer version: I was set up by my former boss to take the fall for some fraudulent accounting schemes and was eventually cleared by a tech-savvy SEC officer. There was a nice settlement, I didn't have to pay any legal fees, and they even offered my job back. But I had gotten such a bad taste in my mouth for the company that going back didn't seem like such a great idea. I think the executives, the ones who didn't get convicted, that is, were happy that I wasn't going to be around. They didn't want to be reminded either.

"Anyway, about a year after that, my wife got breast cancer, and we lost her within six months. Losing my job was a walk in the park compared to the last half of that year.

"Needless to say, I experienced a bit of an existential crisis, so I started taking night classes like these to see if I can't sort through this.

"So ... what's important to me? Awhile back, I gave up on trying to find a reason for all these things going on. I guess all I really need now is the confidence that some sort of reason exists, even though I may never know what it is."

"My name is Patricia Schoff, and I'm a single mom. My son's name is Ryan, and he's eight years old now. I paid my gas bill this month; that's important to me. I'm finishing my degree so I can tell Flirty Fred, my current boss, to go take a hike; that's really important to me. I'm taking this class because I want to learn more about how different people think—and if I learn anything, maybe pass some of that along to Ryan."

"My name is Cathy Williams, and I'm here because I like to talk."

"OK, I'll go next. My name is Kevin Malone, and I don't have a lot of patience for small talk. Get to your point quickly, and we'll be best friends. I'm passionate about fighting censorship in any form; I think it's arrogant for anyone to think they need to filter information to make it more palatable for me. Forget that. So I'm here to learn more about what may have been 'hidden' from me by well-intentioned teachers."

"My name is Sonia Lee, and I *love* to chitchat; and it'll probably take me awhile to get to my point. Sometimes I don't know what my point is. I love spending time with my friends and my mom.

It made me shiver, and I about made up my mind to pray and see if I couldn't try to quit being the kind of boy I was and be better. So I kneeled down. But the words wouldn't come. Why wouldn't they? It weren't no use to try and hide it from Him.... I knowed very well why they wouldn't come. It was because my heart wasn't right; it was because I was playin' double. I was lettin' on to give up sin, but way inside of me I was holdin' on to the biggest one of all. I was tryin' to make my mouth say I would do the right thing and the clean thing, but deep down in me I knowed it was a lie and He knowed it. You can't pray a lie. I found that out.

—MARK TWAIN, *ADVENTURES OF HUCKLEBERRY FINN*

The mall is my sanctuary, and I get reenergized when I shop. I don't like spending time alone, so I'm usually around people. And that reminds me, are we going to pass around e-mail addresses and cell numbers?"

"Sure, for those who want to share that information." Jacob knew that after a few weeks, people usually offered their contact info.

"Great! I look forward to getting to know everybody."

"My name is Kim Prescott. I've been married for seven years and have two kids. I'm not afraid to talk about anything, but if the conversation starts going south in terms of mutual respect, I'm going to excuse myself. Kindness is important to me."

"I'm Regina Shire. You'll have to excuse me if I come across as a little blunt. I'm not as concerned about people's feelings as I am about what's true. Like Kim, I'm not going to tolerate any personal attacks—but it doesn't seem to me like that's going to be a problem. I'm here to understand people, and perhaps myself, a bit better. That's what's important to me."

"My name is Jacob Prevedel. I'm a systems analyst during the day, and at night I like to be involved here—either with the class or preparing for it. I deeply value a rich inner life, and you're in this class because it's the opinion of your other teachers that you share these values."

As usual, that raised a few eyebrows.

"I love this class because it deliberately pits one worldview against another—and I love to see who wins. Again, I try to be neutral in these discussions and hold my cards close to my chest. I already know what I believe. My satisfaction in this class will come from listening to you. So speak often and freely.

"As you see from the schedule, the first couple of classes are short and introductory. We'll be getting deeper into our discussions next week.

"Here are the quotes representing the two worldviews we'll be discussing:

"'Happiness resides not in possessions and not in gold, the feeling of happiness dwells in the soul,' Democritus.[4] 'Greed is right. Greed works. Greed clarifies, cuts through, and captures the essence of the evolutionary spirit. Greed, in all of its forms—greed for life, for money, for love, knowledge—has marked the upward surge of mankind,' Gordon Gekko, the character played by Michael Douglas in the movie *Wall Street*."[5]

> MAKE EVERY EFFORT TO ADD TO YOUR FAITH GOODNESS.
>
> 2 PETER 1:5

CHAPTER 6

GOODNESS:

Engaging a Hostile Culture without Losing Your Identity

GOODNESS: 1. THE STATE OR QUALITY OF BEING GOOD.

GOOD: 1. BEING POSITIVE OR DESIRABLE IN NATURE. 2. SERVING THE DESIRED PURPOSE OR END; SUITABLE. 3. NOT SPOILED OR RUINED. 4. IN EXCELLENT CONDITION; SOUND. 5. WORTHY OF RESPECT; HONORABLE. 6. COMPETENT; SKILLED. 7. RELIABLE; SURE. 8. GENUINE; REAL. 9. ABLE TO CONTRIBUTE. 10. ABLE TO ELICIT A SPECIFIED REACTION. 11. PLEASANT; ENJOYABLE. 12. OF MORAL EXCELLENCE.

DICTIONARY.COM

How do you stay good in a world that is fully committed to dishonoring God and stopping the advancement of his dominion?

Like most kids, my oldest daughter faces remarkable peer pressure in school. Surprisingly though, the pressure isn't about drugs, sex, or cheating (though we expect those issues will come). Instead, she's asked repeatedly why she bothers believing in God (much less, why she is a Christian). Why can't an all-powerful God do the impossible (like make a rock so big he can't lift it)? Or how can you believe God is good when there's so much suffering in the world?

"Dad, I don't know how to answer them. What do I say?" she's lamented.

Peter makes it clear that the traits of spiritual growth build upon each other ("make every effort to add to your faith goodness; and to goodness, knowledge" [2 Peter 1:5]). Of course, in many ways, these traits are like the fruit of the Spirit (see Gal. 5:22–23). All are usually present at the same time, but some can be stronger than others, and one can build upon and strengthen another.

It's interesting to note that Peter places goodness after faith but before knowledge. Usually the right thing to do is obvious, and we usually do it without knowing the reason behind doing so. In fact, doing the right thing might initially seem to be illogical.

In my daughter's case, she needed to practice goodness around her secular friends, showing them kindness and respect, before giving them an articulate response to their paltry and flimsy excuses for ignoring God.

Yes, I did buy my daughter a thick apologetics book that provided gracious but articulate responses to the difficult questions that her friends were posing. She was encouraged to see that these so-called theological dilemmas had been presented before and that there were resources out there to help her respond to them.

But what I encouraged her to do was simply listen and ask her friends to take their beliefs to their logical conclusions. For example, "Why should we follow any rules, and why should we be treated fairly if God does not exist? If there's no standard for defining what is 'good,' why should we follow yours?"

And once they knew they had been heard, they wanted to know what she believed.

Part of the trust-building process with God concerns how we interact with the world. He wants us to practice goodness in a hostile environment, to be able to engage the world without compromising or losing our identity in Christ. This is what it means to be *in* the world but not *of* the world.

IN, NOT OF THE WORLD

Jesus addressed this issue in the parable of the dishonest steward, which seems to end in a mild rebuke to his disciples:

> Jesus told his disciples: "There was a rich man whose manager was accused of wasting his possessions. So he called him in and asked him, 'What is this I hear about you? Give an account of your management, because you cannot be manager any longer.'
>
> "The manager said to himself, 'What shall I do now? My master is taking away my job. I'm not strong enough to dig, and I'm ashamed to beg—I know what I'll do so that, when I lose my job here, people will welcome me into their houses.'
>
> "So he called in each one of his master's debtors. He asked the first, 'How much do you owe my master?'
>
> "'Eight hundred gallons of olive oil,' he replied.
>
> "The manager told him, 'Take your bill, sit down quickly, and make it four hundred.'
>
> "Then he asked the second, 'And how much do you owe?'
>
> "'A thousand bushels of wheat,' he replied.
>
> "He told him, 'Take your bill and make it eight hundred.'
>
> "The master commended the dishonest manager because he had acted shrewdly. *For the people of this world are more shrewd in dealing with their own kind than are the people of the light.*" (Luke 16:1–8)

Like in the parable of the widow and the unjust judge (see Luke 18:1–8), Jesus was setting up a contrast between the main characters and God and his followers. Jesus clearly wants us to be shrewd like the dishonest manager—minus the dishonesty, mediocrity, and incompetence.

But Jesus didn't end the lesson there. He seems to have expressed a small degree of frustration with the inability of those who are "of the light" to deal effectively with the people of the world. When it comes to interacting with culture that is antifaith and morally fluid, what does it mean to be as "wise as serpents, and harmless as doves" (Matt. 10:16 KJV)?

To answer this question, we need to find a good role model. Biblically speaking, there's probably no stronger role model in the arena of effectively engaging a faith-hostile culture than Daniel.

Let's begin our study of this master of culture engagement by looking at God's opinion of Daniel as expressed by the angel Gabriel toward the end of the Daniel's life.

> [Gabriel] ... said to me, "Daniel, I have now come to give you insight and understanding. As soon as you began to pray, an answer was given, which I have come to tell you, for *you are highly esteemed.*" (Dan. 9:22–23)

Some five hundred years later, this same angel told a young woman that she was also highly esteemed by God—and then she was entrusted with raising the most significant human being who ever walked the face of the earth—God the Son.

Probably the highest words of praise and esteem were those pronounced by God at Jesus' baptism: "You are my Son ... with you I am well pleased" (Luke 3:22).

In all of the cases, to be "highly esteemed," "well pleas[ing]," or "highly favored" by God means to be supremely trusted by him. In Daniel's case, he was not only charged with bearing testimony of the living God to two superpowers, but also entrusted with visions of how history would unfold and eventually end.

Daniel is one of the few characters of whom the Bible says nothing negative. He truly is one our best representatives of what Peter means by "goodness." In fact, even his enemies couldn't find any dirty laundry about him:

KINGDOM SPOTLIGHT

KINGDOM MIXING

As we talked about, when the Devil tempted Jesus in the wilderness, he made an assertion that the Lord neither confirmed nor denied:

> The devil led him up to a high place and showed him in an instant all the kingdoms of the world. And he said to him, "I will give you all their authority and splendor, for it has been given to me, and I can give it to anyone I want to." (Luke 4:5–7)

While there is no direct biblical reference to God giving Satan the kingdom of the world, the Prince of Darkness seemed to waste no time claiming it, and God seemed to expend no effort to prevent it.

Because of this apparent arrangement, Jesus made it clear that until "the kingdoms of men had become of the kingdoms of our God" (see Rev. 11:15) there would be some "kingdom mixing," in which friend and foe coexisted until the final day.

Jesus illustrated this in the parable of the tares and the wheat. The word *tares* was generally used to describe any type of weed, but the noxious plant that Jesus probably had in mind was the bearded darnel. It looked deceptively like wheat.

> Jesus told them another parable: "The kingdom of heaven is like a man who sowed good seed in his field. But while everyone was sleeping, his enemy came and sowed weeds among the wheat [a crime under Roman law], and went away. When the wheat sprouted and formed heads, then the weeds also appeared.
>
> "The owner's servants came to him and said, 'Sir, didn't you sow good seed in your field? Where then did the weeds come from?'
>
> "'An enemy did this,' he replied.
>
> "The servants asked him, 'Do you want us to go and pull them up?'
>
> "'No,' he answered, 'because while you are pulling the weeds, you may root up the wheat with them. Let both grow together until the harvest. At that time I will tell the harvesters: First collect the weeds and tie them in bundles to be burned; then gather the wheat and bring it into my barn.'" (Matt. 13:24–30)

Because of the possible danger to those who belong to God, the Lord holds off on the weeding process until the edible plants are fully ripe. In the meantime, the Lord expects us to find a way to coexist with these rebellious folks, because he isn't going to intervene (in a massive way) until he returns.

The administrators and the satraps tried to find grounds for charges against Daniel in his conduct of government affairs, but they were unable to do so. They could find no corruption in him, because he was trustworthy and neither corrupt nor negligent. (Dan. 6:4)

Daniel's introduction to a culture very different from his own was involuntary. During the reign of Jehoiakim, king of Judah, the Babylonian monarch Nebuchadnezzar besieged Jerusalem and carried off some of Judah's young men for service in his court. These hostages included Shadrach, Meshach, Abednego, and Daniel. Daniel was probably in his teens when he was captured. Since Daniel's story ends during the time of Darius the Mede, it seems that Daniel spent more than eighty years in captivity and never returned to his homeland.

Like Cain, Balaam, Hagar, and Naaman, Nebuchadnezzar was also an unbeliever with whom God had a personal relationship. Because of Nebuchadnezzar's proclamations at the end of his life, we can be fairly assured that this once most powerful man in the world was eventually reconciled with the living God.

Because of Daniel's goodness, namely his ability to engage a hostile culture without compromising his identity in Christ, he was clearly used by God to facilitate this spiritual transition for the Babylonian king.

How did he successfully do this?

First, he was able to immerse himself in the culture without being unduly influenced by it:

> The king ordered Ashpenaz, chief of his court officials ... to teach them the language and literature of the Babylonians.... To these four young men God gave knowledge and understanding of all kinds of literature and learning. And Daniel could understand visions and dreams of all kinds. (Dan. 1:3–4, 17)

The language and literature of Babylon, at the time, were steeped in mythology, historical lies, and barbarian cruelty. The Babylonians' savagery was exceeded only by that of the Assyrians. Even so, this knowledge gave Daniel and his companions the necessary knowledge to build bridges with their oppressors and to remain articulate witnesses for the living God.

We see this level of education also in the apostle Paul, who was clearly familiar with foreign literature and poetry and on several occasions used this knowledge as a bridge for the gospel. And the first Christian martyr, Stephen, reminds us that Moses had a similar experience growing up in an ungodly culture: "Moses was educated in all the wisdom of the Egyptians and was powerful in speech and action" (Acts 7:22).

Second, Daniel knew when to compromise, when to simply not respond, and when to draw the line when he was clearly being pushed to disobey God's commands.

Surprisingly, Daniel and his friends were given the Babylonian names without any evidence of protest. And they were named after some Babylonian gods! (At least no such protest is recorded in the text, and these four were not hesitant to take a stand when it mattered, so we can reasonably assume that the four simply didn't fight the names that were given to them.)

On the other hand, Daniel does introduce us to the first dramatic "Veggie Tale" in the Bible. Nebuchadnezzar insisted that his protégés eat of the king's table. The menu obviously included items that were considered unclean by the Jews. To partake of these particular foods would be a ceremonial defilement for Daniel and his friends—and this was a compromise that they were not willing to make.

So Daniel, upon the risk of death, suggested a middle ground. He proposed a test between the four of them and the other captives. He suggested that he and his friends eat only foods that were compatible with their Jewish heritage (vegetables and water) while the other men ate the king's unclean food, and then they would see who fared better. Well, Daniel and his group looked better at the end of the test, so the king made Daniel's faith-based standard the new Babylonian rule for preparing the king's servants.

Several years later, Daniel passed a similar test after Babylon fell to the Medes and the Persians. (Hostile takeovers are not limited to the contemporary corporate world; they've been going on for centuries, and the people of God simply move along with them.) During this time, Daniel had a habit of daily prayer that he was expected to give up as an expression of devotion and worship of the Persian king. Again, Daniel knew where to draw the line, even when his enemies had the upper hand. Because of his stand, Daniel was thrown into a den of hungry lions, but he was saved by the hand of God. This display of God's power resulted in another pagan king acknowledging the sovereignty of the living God.

When Shadrach, Meshach, and Abednego faced their own trial, their expression of trust in God had a twist that you do not hear of very often these days. Like Daniel, these three knew where to draw the line. When required to bow down to a statue of Nebuchadnezzar as an act of worship, they kept standing. After facing the fiery anger of the jilted king, they gave an interesting response:

> O Nebuchadnezzar, we do not need to defend ourselves before you in this matter. If we are thrown into the blazing furnace, the God we serve *is able* to save us from it, and he will rescue us from your hand, O king. *But even if he does not*, we want you to know, O king, that we will not serve your gods or worship the image of gold you have set up. (Dan. 3:16–18)

Wow! In essence they were saying, "We have faith that our God is able to do anything, even get us out of this bind. But even if he does not, we will not compromise our identity or association with him." It's interesting to note that trusting God for these three young

> Jesus evidently felt deeply the emptiness and futility of much ... religious talk. He was interested only in those emotions and professions which could get themselves translated into character and action. Words have always been the bane of religion as well as its vehicle. Religious emotion has enormous motive force, but it is the easiest thing in the world for it to sizzle away in high professions and wordy prayers. In that case, it is a substitute and counterfeit, and a damage to the Reign of God among men.
>
> —WALTER RAUSCHENBUSCH
> THE SOCIAL PRINCIPLES OF JESUS (1916)

men did not mean that they were trusting God to prevent their execution. They were trusting God to get them through whatever the consequences of their obedience turned out to be. Their faith is reminiscent of Job's cry after pouring out his frustration: "Though he slay me, yet will I [trust] him" (Job 13:15). As we will see later, many godly people in the Bible experienced significant losses without losing the affection and love of God. Any experience in life is an opportunity to build, lose, or regain God's trust, regardless of the temporal success or failure.

Once again, God performed a miracle. In this case, he was able *and* willing to deliver them from this fiery trial. And once again, it resulted in the praise of God from a man who had been seeking worship for himself.

> Then Nebuchadnezzar said, "Praise be to the God of Shadrach, Meshach and Abednego, who has sent his angel and rescued his servants! They trusted in him and defied the king's command and were willing to give up their lives rather than serve or worship any god except their own God." (Dan. 3:28)

Finally, Daniel was known for his goodness in a hostile culture because he was clearly identified by those outside the fold as a man of God who was filled with the Holy Spirit. Granted, the Babylonians reflected their mythology when they said of Daniel, "He had the spirit of the gods within him" (see Dan. 5:14). But as we see by Nebuchadnezzar's frequent expression of worship for the God of Israel, he eventually got the biblical idea.

From Daniel's example, we see that it's possible to be engaged with a culture, to learn that culture's language and practice, without becoming so absorbed by it that we are indistinguishable from those who have not been reconciled with God.

Nor are we to be so separate that we can relate only to fellow like-minded believers and not be able to effectively function in the world.

Can you imagine Daniel, Shadrach, Meshach, and Abednego staying in a "holy huddle," unwilling to venture forth and engage their oppressors? If they did, they probably wouldn't have lasted a week.

Exodus versus Exile

Craig Detweiler and Barry Taylor, in their groundbreaking book, *A Matrix of Meanings: Finding God in Pop Culture*, make reference to a lecture they heard at Fuller Theological Seminary by Alan Roxburgh. Roxburgh claimed that many Christians in the West view themselves as an exodus people, trying to escape from an oppressive culture and march forward to the Promised Land. In contrast, Roxburgh claimed that perhaps we are better described as people in exile who must learn to live within the power, predominance, and patronizing attitude of the surrounding culture.

To build on this contrast, I would say that the exodus Christians identify best with Joshua and leaders like him who are out to conquer and dominate the pagan cultures around them. During Joshua's time, this was the right thing to do. God was demonstrating his

NEBUCHADNEZZAR: AN UNLIKELY BELIEVER

Nebuchadnezzar was clearly used by God and raised up by God to be an instrument of discipline for his wayward people. But, of course, God's concern for this man's soul did not end there.

> But because our fathers angered the God of heaven, he handed them over to Nebuchadnezzar the Chaldean, king of Babylon, who destroyed this temple and deported the people to Babylon. (Ezra 5:12)

> "I will summon all the peoples of the north and *my servant* Nebuchadnezzar king of Babylon," declares the LORD, "and I will bring them against this land and its inhabitants and against all the surrounding nations. I will completely destroy them and make them an object of horror and scorn, and an everlasting ruin." (Jer. 25:9)

God called even one who refused to acknowledge him his "servant." In the kingdom of God, you fulfill one of two roles, both in the servant category: pawn or (willing) participant. Nothing escapes God's notice. No one goes unused by him.

> Now I will hand all your countries over to my servant Nebuchadnezzar king of Babylon; I will make even the wild animals subject to him. (Jer. 27:6)

As we'll see later, Daniel had a profound influence upon Nebuchadnezzar. Because of Daniel's ability to engage the pagan Babylonian culture without compromising his relationship with the living God, Nebuchadnezzar—who was during this time the most powerful man in the world—slowly started coming around to seeing things God's way.

---

sovereignty and authority through a people group that he chose, not because of its righteousness or extraordinary qualifications, but to demonstrate his power and grace.

But when those people started looking, acting, and feeling no

> Then King Nebuchadnezzar fell prostrate before Daniel and paid him honor and ordered that an offering and incense be presented to him. (Dan. 2:46)

But then almost immediately afterward ...

> King Nebuchadnezzar made an image of gold, ninety feet high and nine feet wide, and set it up on the plain of Dura in the province of Babylon. (Dan. 3:1)

Like Pharaoh of the exodus, this powerful king kept changing this mind. And yet God demonstrated infinite patience with him. The straw that broke the king's back was that of taking full credit for his success and not acknowledging God. He failed to acknowledge the indisputable truth that Jesus told Pilate just before the Lord was crucified: that those who are in power are there only because they were given this position of authority by God (see John 19:11). So Nebuchadnezzar temporarily lost not only his kingdom, but also his sanity. When he recovered, he finally acknowledged God's sovereignty.

> At the end of that time, I, Nebuchadnezzar, raised my eyes toward heaven, and my sanity was restored. Then I praised the Most High; I honored and glorified him who lives forever. His dominion is an eternal dominion; his kingdom endures from generation to generation. All the peoples of the earth are regarded as nothing. He does as he pleases with the powers of heaven and the peoples of the earth. No one can hold back his hand or say to him: "What have you done?" (Dan. 4:34–35)

different from the ones they conquered, God sent them into exile—and the people of God have been in exile ever since.

Since 586 BC, when Nebuchadnezzar took Zedekiah and gouged out his eyes, the people of God have always been in the minority in

The sad fact is that all Christians are susceptible to worldly wiles. In fact, sad to say, the church has managed to shoot itself in the foot almost every time it has achieved power in society. So what we need most right now is a bracing dose of humility. We're not a labor union, lining up for our share of the spoils after the election. We are the church. Our job is to bring biblical truth to bear in society; to win people to Christ; and to promote righteousness and justice. We serve the King of kings, no mere temporal king.

—Chuck Colson, *BreakPoint*

---

a culture that has much more power, much more influence, than they ever had.

The only time the people of God have been distinctly in the position of "superpower" was during the reigns of David and Solomon—and that quickly collapsed when the power went to their heads; they divided as a nation and then were eventually sent into exile.

So instead of Joshua, perhaps our role model should be Daniel, who was able to fully engage the surrounding culture and yet not lose his identity. I think God prefers us to be in the crucible of the minority (political) power so he can accomplish extraordinary things through our weakness. Again, Daniel is the extreme example of what it means to live in the exile, to demonstrate the goodness of God when perhaps there is little good to be found.

As we've seen in the parable of the shrewd steward, Jesus wants us to know how the world thinks and acts. We can learn from other "kingdoms" without imitating their immorality or failure to acknowledge God's sovereignty. Some of them have learned to do things exceptionally well; they're motivated to do so because this life is all they have to live for.

Certainly a modern-day person of faith who has accomplished this is Condoleezza Rice, former national security advisor to the president and then secretary of state. Talk about a sheep among wolves (both foreign and domestic)! Condoleezza's mother named her after an Italian musical phrase, *con dolcezza*, which means "to perform with sweetness." As an expert in Soviet politics, Rice knew how politically atheistic minds thought, and because of that expertise she was eventually invited to join the National Security Council. When the terrorists struck on September 11, 2001, Rice first called her aunt and uncle from the bunker to tell them that she was all right, and then she started calling heads of state. As one of the most powerful people in the world, she's often asked where she finds her strength, and she replies, "For me it comes from a deep and abiding faith in Jesus Christ."[1]

> *The church is an organism that grows best in an alien society.*
>
> —C. STACEY WOODS

No compromise there. And yet, is there anyone in the world more fully engaged with a multitude of cultures not only hostile to democracy, but even more important, antagonistic to the claims of Christ? Oh, that my daughters will have the same courage when they venture out into the world!

So let's not be afraid to "plunder the Egyptians" when it comes to dealing with worldly matters so that Jesus will not say of us, "The people of this world are more shrewd in dealing with their own kind than are the people of the light" (Luke 16:8). He certainly would have never said that of Daniel—or Condoleezza Rice.

Jesus ends the parable of the dishonest steward with these words:

> Whoever can be trusted with very little can also be trusted with much, and whoever is dishonest with very little will also be dishonest with much. So if you have not been trustworthy in handling worldly wealth, who will trust you with true riches? And if you have not been

trustworthy with someone else's property, who will give you property of your own? (Luke 16:10–12)

So let us focus on gaining God's trust in the little things so that one day he will trust us with enormous (and deeply satisfying) responsibilities.

THE CLASS, PART 3

"All right, glad to see you all made it in. That's the thing about night classes: We usually don't get snow days."

Jacob brushed the snow off his black trench coat and hung it in the usual place.

"Let's start discussing the quotes we passed out last week. 'Happiness resides not in possessions and not in gold, the feeling of happiness dwells in the soul,' Democritus. 'Greed is right. Greed works. Greed clarifies, cuts through, and captures the essence of the evolutionary spirit. Greed, in all of its forms—greed for life, for money, for love, knowledge—has marked the upward surge of mankind,' Gordon Gekko.

"Any response to the Democritus quote?"

Kevin was the first to open his mouth; Jacob could tell this was going to be a pattern.

"Rubbish."

"Any other details you'd like to add, Kevin?"

"It's the concession of a man who hasn't made it, so he's trying to cope with his failure with the ol' sour grapes mantra of the poor: 'Sure, they may be rich, but are they happy?'

"Trust me, I've met a lot of rich people in my time, and they're plenty happy. And if they're not, they've got the resources to numb the pain.

"Gekko, on the other hand, knows how the real world works. Greed is what motivates any successful person. That's the way of the world. Sorry, folks. The sooner people accept that, the better off they'll be."

Sonia was next. "I think most people look out for their best interests before all others, but I wouldn't necessarily call that greed. And as the *Wall Street* movie portrayed, Gekko only got away with it for so long before he was nailed for insider trading. Greed may work for a time, but it creates blind spots."

Kevin's grin, while it didn't go away, sobered up a little.

Ron chimed in. "I think contentment and the desire to grow are mutually exclusive. You can have one or the other, but not both."

Cathy was not going to let that slide. "With all due respect, Ron, that's nonsense. I think contentment and growth go in cycles; sometimes one gets more attention than the other. If we're always driving, driving, driving for more and never enjoy what we have, what's the use? And if we become so content that we never try to stretch ourselves, well, that's a waste of time too. There's got to be some way to balance the two."

As Jacob expected, the conversation was lively for the next ninety minutes, and everyone seemed to be getting more comfortable with one another. As nine o'clock approached, Jacob decided to wrap things up for the evening.

"OK, for your next assignment please check out one or more of the following books, and generate some questions that the authors provoke. No kid gloves here; put the authors to task. Please hand your questions in at the beginning of the next class session.

"Here are the books: *The Plague* by Albert Camus, *Who Am I? The 16 Basic Desires That Motivate Our Actions and Define Our Personalities* by Steven Reiss, *Father Joe: The Man Who Saved My Soul* by Tony Hendra, *You Can Take It with You!* by Doug Schmidt, *The Prince* by Niccolo Machiavelli, and *A Matrix of Meanings* by Craig Detweiler and Barry Taylor.

"And here are the quotes we'll be chasing around next week: "'Power is of two kinds. One is obtained by the fear of punishment and the other by acts of love. Power based on love is a thousand times more effective and permanent then [sic] the one derived from fear of punishment,' Mohandas K. Gandhi.[2] 'Since love and fear can hardly exist together, if we must choose between them, it is far safer to be feared than loved,' Niccolo Machiavelli."[3]

MAKE EVERY EFFORT TO ADD TO YOUR ... GOODNESS, KNOWLEDGE.

2 PETER 1:5

Chapter 7

Knowledge:
A Genuine Desire to Understand

KNOWLEDGE: 1. The state or fact of knowing. 2. Familiarity, awareness, or understanding gained through experience or study. 3. Specific information about something. 4. The sum or range of what has been perceived, discovered, or learned.

Dictionary.com

[Jesus] said, "The knowledge of the secrets of the kingdom of God has been given to you, but to others I speak in parables, so that, 'though seeing, they may not see; though hearing, they may not understand.'"
Luke 8:10

I remember as a young Christian wondering why Jesus wouldn't want someone to understand what he was teaching. Wouldn't it be better for people to understand it and reject it than to simply dismiss it because they could not grasp what he was saying?

Apparently not! Genuine knowledge about the kingdom was something that Jesus reserved for those *who genuinely desired to know God*. For this reason he often spoke in parables.

Do you remember what happened after Jesus fed the five thousand, as told in John 6:1–14? The crowds were so enamored with Jesus' obvious power that they attempted to "make him king by force"

> Jesus talked to them in parables, confusing stories that required considerable effort to process. The teeming crowd began to thin as those who had come merely for the show were forced to think. No doubt many walked away thinking, "Fun's over. This guy speaks in senseless riddles. I gotta get back to work." The group that remained, possibly much smaller than the original, willingly struggled with the imagery, desperately seeking the answer.... Jesus told parables to sift the crowd, separating out the hard-hearted from those who had the heart to understand. He didn't tell parables because all people were deaf to them. He told parables to separate those seeking truth in God and willing to make the effort from the carnival goers with selfish hearts.
> —MICHAEL SIMPSON, *PERMISSION EVANGELISM*

(v. 15). Jesus would have none of it. He simply withdrew from them—no more bread, no more teaching, no more miracles for that group. Perhaps it is the often negative, greedy reaction to miracles that holds the Lord back from offering them, even when one is sorely needed.

KNOWLEDGE: ENTRUSTED OR NOT

God loves the world deeply, but he simply cannot trust those with whom he has not been reconciled. Consider the painful dilemma of seemingly irreconcilable conflict. Though we may still love those with whom we have been estranged, it's usually neither prudent nor wise to trust them. Intimate information about us will either be treated with painful indifference or exploited to expose our vulnerability—and perhaps those we care about.

Jesus hinted at this problem when he advised his followers not to throw pearls in front of pigs, because if you do, they may trample them under their feet and then turn and tear you to pieces (see Matt. 7:6). It's bad enough how some people twist the plain teaching of Scripture for their own ends. The Holy Spirit apparently hides these truths from people who, at this point, he does not consider trustworthy.

> The secret things belong to the LORD our God, but the things revealed belong to us and to our children forever, that we may follow all the words of this law. (Deut. 29:29)

God keeps secrets. Some things will always remain a mystery, things that God keeps to himself, concepts that might overwhelm us if we were to merely get an inkling of what's behind them. At one point during his ministry, Jesus told his disciples, "I have many things to teach you, but you can't bear them now" (see John 16:12). When it comes to spiritual growth, there are many things that we will eventually know (according to the wisdom of the Holy Spirit), but right now we may not have the tools to understand them. Those who want to know more about the kingdom will discover those things God is willing to reveal. If you want to know, you'll find the answer. It takes only a little digging, and if you still don't get it, keep asking until you get the answers you seek. But if you don't really want to understand, you'll probably never grasp the full implications of what Jesus is trying to tell us here about the kingdom.

Jesus told us these things because he really wants us to know (if we're up for the lessons). Certainly he wanted the disciples to know, but even they had their moments. In Mark 8, Jesus mildly rebuked his followers for still not "getting it." He used language that alludes to the Isaiah passage he quoted above (in Luke 8:10).

> "Be careful," Jesus warned them. "Watch out for the yeast of the Pharisees and that of Herod."
>
> They discussed this with one another and said, "It is because we have no bread."
>
> Aware of their discussion, Jesus asked them: "Why are you talking about having no bread? Do you still not see or understand? Are your hearts hardened? Do you have eyes but fail to see, and ears but fail to hear? And don't you remember?" (Mark 8:15–18)

Jesus was patient with them, and eventually they did get it because their hearts softened. So for those whose hearts are in a state of readiness to learn, to those who are committed to gaining God's trust, these truths will be revealed. And this is the type of knowledge that Peter wants us to have. To this end, let's take a closer look at "the knowledge of the secrets of the kingdom of God" that Jesus taught us through his kingdom parables.

The Kingdom of God Is Like ...

... a treasure hidden in a field or a merchant looking for fine pearls.

> The kingdom of heaven is like treasure hidden in a field. When a man found it, he hid it again, and then in his joy went and sold all he had and bought that field. (Matt. 13:44)

> Again, the kingdom of heaven is like a merchant looking for fine pearls. When he found one of great value, he went away and sold everything he had and bought it. (Matt. 13:45–46)

People who do not value what God has provided for them are not going to seek him or his kingdom. Those who do recognize the kingdom's value are ready to let go of everything they once held dear in order to make it their own. Once a person realizes the infinite value of something compared to the little they have in their hands, suddenly they're ready to give up everything in order to obtain it. Any sacrifice is worth it.

No one is forcing this kingdom upon us. As we saw earlier, even Jesus resisted being made King. You need to voluntarily trade one thing for another.

When we discuss Peter's trait of self-control, we'll talk about what it means to give up our "minikingdoms" ("everything [we have]") in order to submit and integrate into God's kingdom.

SECRET HEAVENLY IDENTITIES

"He who has an ear, let him hear what the Spirit says to the churches. To him who overcomes, I will give some of the hidden manna. I will also give him a white stone with a new name written on it, known only to him who receives it" (Rev. 2:17).

Since there are names in heaven that only the recipients know, it follows that we will not know everything in heaven.

The passage in Corinthians that mentions seeing through a glass darkly and then seeing face-to-face (see 1 Cor. 13:12) simply means that certain mysteries will be cleared up. But it does not mean we will become omniscient, knowing everything. We are created beings, and while our knowledge base will grow exponentially in the Final Dominion, we will clearly not know everything. Only God could handle such a characteristic without becoming insanely bored.

So I speculate that there will be much to discover in the Final Dominion and magnificent things to create from that which we do discover.

A KING WHO PREPARED A WEDDING BANQUET FOR HIS SON

> When the king came in to see the guests, he noticed a man there who was not wearing wedding clothes. "Friend," he asked, "how did you get in here without wedding clothes?" The man was speechless.
>
> Then the king told the attendants, "Tie him hand and foot, and throw him outside, into the darkness, where there will be weeping and gnashing of teeth.
>
> "For many are invited, but few are chosen." (Matt. 22:11–14)

Many kids are under enormous pressure to spend incredible amounts of money on clothes. And some just don't care; they look neat, spend what is reasonable, and remain respected. But people are not getting into school wearing nothing but a swimsuit—or at least they won't be staying for very long if they do. You have to have the right clothes.

KINGDOM SPOTLIGHT

GOD INSPIRES, MAN CREATES

God made hummingbirds as small as bees and whales as big as buses, chameleons that can change to any color, sloths that grow moss on their backs, parrots that can talk and swifts that sleep while they are flying, moths that look like leaves and insects that look like sticks, skunks that smell disgusting (except to other skunks), squirrels that fly, bees that dance, worms that eat mud and goats that eat anything, dolphins that smile, crocodiles that grin and hyenas that laugh, butterflyfish and parrotfish and lionfish and batfish and catfish and dogfish and hogfish, hairy caterpillars and bold eagles, beavers that build dams and moles that dig tunnels, kangaroos that carry their babies in pouches and pelicans with beaks like shopping bags, sharks with teeth like razors, beetles with antlers, gorillas as strong as ten men, jumping fleas and jumping spiders, toads that blow themselves up like balloons, electric eels and beetles that glow in the dark, bears that sleep all winter long, termites that make tall houses as tough as concrete, salmon that can swim up waterfalls, lizards like dragons, elephants with noses like hoses and squids that squirt ink. He made animals that sing and squawk and spout and hiss and hoot and howl and honk and chirp and peck and pounce and flap and fly and slide and slither and squirm and creep and crawl and prowl and growl and gallop and glide and dive and swoop and jump and hang and warble and squeak and roar. He made a whole lot of animals you have probably never heard of ... the dugong, the common noddy, the slow loris, the wrestling halfbeak, the weedy seadragon, the pink fairy armadillo, the rubber boa, the football fish, the banana quit, and the bush squeaker.

—Nick Butterworth and Mick Inkpen[1]

Inspired by God's creation, people in turn created alphabets, animation, answering machines, aspirin, Astroturf, audiotapes, bags, balloons, bandages, bar codes, batteries, bikes, bifocals, blow-dryers, boomerangs, braille, bread, buttons ...

Tell all the skilled men to whom I have given wisdom in such matters ... (Ex. 28:3)

... calculus, calendars, cameras, candles, cans, cardboard, cellophane, cereal, chocolate, clocks, coffee, CDs, compasses, computers, concrete, contact paper, correction fluid, cotton gins, crayons, crossword puzzles, defibrillators, diapers, DVDs, dishwashers, doughnuts, drinking fountains, dry cleaning ...

I have filled him with the Spirit of God, with skill, ability and knowledge in all kinds of crafts. (Ex. 31:3)

... elastic, electrocardiograms, elevators, engines, fax machines, fiber optics, flashlights, fusion, glass, guitars, hangers, insulin, Jell-O, Kevlar, lawn mowers ...

> Bless all his skills, O LORD, and be pleased with the work of his hands. (Deut. 33:11)

... lightbulbs, linoleum, locks, magnetic resonance imaging, margarine, microwaves, miniature golf, mirrors, Morse code, nylon, oil lamps, pacemakers, paper, paper clips, paper towels, parachutes, particle accelerators ...

> [The Lord] has filled him with the Spirit of God, with skill, ability and knowledge in all kinds of crafts. (Ex. 35:31)

... pasteurization, pencils, phonographs, photography, Play-Doh, plows, Post-it notes, printing presses, radar, radio, reapers, records, remote controls, respirators, Richter scales, rubber, saddles, safety pins, satellites, saxophones, Scotch tape, seat belts, sewing machines, shoelaces, skates, skiing, snowmobiles, soap, sonar, stamps, staplers, steel, stereos, stoves, straws ...

> Moses summoned Bezalel and Oholiab and every skilled person to whom the LORD had given ability and who was willing to come and do the work. (Ex. 36:2)

... submarines, sunscreen, synthetic skin, tea bags, Teflon, telegraphs, telephones, thermometers, tires, tissue, toasters, toilets, toothbrushes, tractors ...

> [The Lord] has filled them with skill to do all kinds of work as craftsmen, designers, embroiderers in blue, purple and scarlet yarn and fine linen, and weavers—all of them master craftsmen and designers. (Ex. 35:35)

... transistors, typewriters, ultrasound, vaccinations, vacuums, Velcro, video, vision correction, washing machines, the wheel, wheelbarrows, windmills, the World Wide Web, X-rays, and Zambonies.[2]

> I believe that God deliberately created an insanely complex universe so that we could never get to the bottom of interesting things. In a sense, we are his beta fish, and I suppose he could have poured us into a featureless glass bowl with no place to go and not much to look at. But he placed us in an ocean—an endless expanse of scientific, historical, philosophical and spiritual complexities that beckon us to swim around in them and marvel.
>
> —Paul Lundquist, pastor[3]

The same is true for entering into the kingdom of God. You must wear the right thing. Of course, Jesus was using an analogy here and leaving it up to those who really want to know to figure it out.

A clue to the meaning of the metaphor can actually be found in the Old Testament in the small book of Zechariah:

> Then he showed me Joshua the high priest standing before the angel of the Lord, and Satan standing at his right side to accuse him. The Lord said to Satan, "The Lord rebuke you, Satan! The Lord, who has chosen Jerusalem, rebuke you! Is not this man a burning stick snatched from the fire?"
>
> Now Joshua was dressed in filthy clothes as he stood before the angel. The angel said to those who were standing before him, "Take off his filthy clothes."
>
> Then he said to Joshua, "See, I have taken away your sin, and I will put rich garments on you." (3:1–4)

Bottom line, the only acceptable "clothes" come from God. They represent the righteousness given to those whose sin is taken away.

A Seed Planted in the Ground

> He also said, "This is what the kingdom of God is like. A man scatters seed on the ground. Night and day, whether he sleeps or gets up, the seed sprouts and grows, though he does not know how. All by itself the soil produces grain—first the stalk, then the head, then the full kernel in the head. As soon as the grain is ripe, he puts the sickle to it, because the harvest has come." (Mark 4:26–29)

Even though we may not understand the "mechanism" behind spiritual growth, we need to keep moving forward anyway, doing what honors God, no matter how seemingly trivial or mundane. As the process proceeds and eventually concludes, those who are faithful in the planting reap the benefits.

The preacher may seem to have an ... easy task. At first sight, it may seem that they have only to proclaim and declare; but in fact, if their words are to enter men's hearts and bear fruit, they must be the right words, shaped cunningly to pass men's defenses and explode silently and effectually within their minds. This means, in practice, turning a face of flint toward the easy cliché, the well-worn religious cant and phraseology—dear, no doubt, to the faithful, but utterly meaningless to those outside the fold. It means learning how people are thinking and how they are feeling; it means learning with patience, imagination and ingenuity the way to pierce apathy or blank lack of understanding. I sometimes wonder what hours of prayer and thought lie behind the apparently simple and spontaneous parables of the Gospel.

—J. B. PHILLIPS (1906–1982), *MAKING MEN WHOLE* (1952)

> He told them another parable: "The kingdom of heaven is like a mustard seed, which a man took and planted in his field. Though it is the smallest of all your seeds, yet when it grows, it is the largest of garden plants and becomes a tree, so that the birds of the air come and perch in its branches."
> (Matt. 13:31–32)

Remember when Jesus told the disciples that if they had the faith of a mustard seed they could move mountains and uproot trees (see Matt. 17:20)? Jesus mentioned the mustard seed because it was among the smallest of all the seeds. His point was clear: In God's dominion, it doesn't take much to get things going. The mustard plant reaches ten, sometimes fifteen feet in height. In the fall of the year its branches can become rigid, and thus it is able to serve as a shelter for many animals.

So given the final height of a mustard plant, about the distance of a basketball hoop from the gym floor, we can see that the end product is literally millions of times the size of the original seed. Jesus wasn't making a mathematically precise statement here, but

THE MISGUIDED IDEA OF HUMAN OMNISCIENCE

In the Final Dominion, will those who have been reconciled with God know everything?

I must admit that the possibility of human omniscience has caused me no small amount of trepidation. Some of my closest friends would say I might have the spiritual gift of knowledge—which does not necessarily mean that I know a lot, but that I'm constantly wanting to know, that my desire to learn borders on obsession (in a healthy sense, I suppose). I think the sure sign that someone has this gift is that when he finally understands a certain biblical truth, his first response is to worship, because he understands that his capacity to understand anything is utterly dependent on the teaching ministry of the Holy Spirit.

---

he was saying this: As the dominion of God advances, it will become exponentially bigger, both in terms of breadth and depth, than it is right now.

Spiritual growth in God's dominion is a cooperative effort; we plant the seeds, and God mysteriously causes phenomenal growth. (We will address other kingdom parables in later chapters.)

KNOWLEDGE IN SCRIPTURE

There are over 130 references to *knowledge* in the Scriptures. This parable that reveals "the knowledge of the secrets of the kingdom" (Matt. 13:11) only scratches the surface. For example:

> You must not eat from the tree of the knowledge of good and evil, for when you eat of it you will surely die. (Gen. 2:17)

> I have filled him with the Spirit of God, with skill, ability and knowledge in all kinds of crafts. (Ex. 31:3)

Many Christians think that Paul's teaching in the love chapter of 1 Corinthians 13 indicates that when we are in the presence of God we will finally know everything.

> Now we see but a poor reflection as in a mirror; then we shall see face to face. Now I know in part; then I shall know fully, even as I am fully known. (1 Cor. 13:12)

The knowledge that Paul speaks about in this passage is God's knowledge of us as individuals. Because God is omniscient (all-knowing), there is no aspect of our personalities that he is not intimately familiar with. And in this context, "to know fully" is better understood to mean everything that we do know, we will know correctly, not necessarily exhaustively.

Give me wisdom and knowledge, that I may lead this people, for who is able to govern this great people of yours? (2 Chron. 1:10)

Who is this that darkens my counsel with words without knowledge? (Job 38:2)

You asked, "Who is this that obscures my counsel without knowledge?" Surely I spoke of things I did not understand, things too wonderful for me to know. (Job 42:3)

The fear of the Lord is the beginning of knowledge. (Prov. 1:7)

Of course, if you really want to understand the biblical concept of knowledge, you're going to do whatever it takes to get that information. Aren't you?

The person whom God trusts genuinely wants to know more about him and his dominion and will do whatever it takes to get that information and use it in a way that honors God.

The Class: A Final Dialogue

The coffeehouse was surprisingly quiet for a Thursday night. Since the college had started block scheduling, most people began their weekends after the last class on Thursday, and many of them headed for this place. Jacob got there early to save a large enough table for the class, but he didn't need to.

Maybe there's a concert or something tonight, thought Jacob.

The real reason the place was empty had occurred while the professor was driving. He usually kept the radio off during this drive to think about the night's upcoming discussion, so he was unaware of what had happened.

A midsize theater in a rural German town was playing a film that was not too friendly to a certain religious group. About twenty minutes into the movie, a bomb went off from behind the screen. Those who weren't killed by the blast were eventually overcome by the smoke and toxic fumes. Three hundred four people died almost instantaneously. As news of the bombing made its way through the airways, most people just decided to stay in that night, away from the theaters, restaurants, and coffee shops.

Sonia and Patricia were the first ones to arrive, and Jacob could tell by their countenances that something terrible had happened. When everyone had arrived, Jacob suggested they postpone the night's discussion, but they all insisted on moving forward, especially in light of the night's topic: love versus fear.

"OK then," sighed Jacob. "I appreciate your willingness and courage to forge ahead. Let me read the quotes again.

"'Power is of two kinds. One is obtained by the fear of punishment and the other by acts of love. Power based on love is a thousand times more effective and permanent then [sic] the one derived from fear of punishment,' Mohandas K. Gandhi. 'Since love and fear can hardly exist together, if we must choose between them, it is far safer to be feared than loved,' Niccolo Machiavelli."

"I don't know," said Patricia. "Fear is a pretty powerful motivating force—especially now that I'm feeling it in every pore of my body. With this kind of terror hanging over my head, it's hard to feel loving or to believe that I'll ever be treated in a loving way. I'm sure once things settle down, I'll feel different, but for now, I'd do whatever a terrorist told me to do just so he wouldn't hurt me or my son."

Sonia was nervously tapping her fingers on the table. "I think in a few days my fear is going to turn into anger, and I'm not going to feel very loving or trusting either."

"At the risk of sounding very insensitive," Ron offered quietly, "I believe that the reason people like Gandhi, King, and others who thought love was more effective than fear is that they weren't afraid to lose anything, even their lives. Most tyrants who use fear to motivate others look for what people fear to lose most and then level their weapons on that particular monument, reputation, or person. Take away the paralyzing anxiety of potential loss, and fear—at least as a motivating force—becomes impotent."

Kevin's fear had already turned into anger. It had taken all of about seven seconds after he heard the first news reports. "As you've probably figured out by now, I'm no Mahatma Gandhi or Martin Luther King. I simply don't have the patience to analyze and inventory what I'm willing to lose in order for fear to lose its sting.

"Most people are more Machiavellian than they care to admit. Whether or not they claim to believe in moral absolutes, they're quite flexible in their standards when something is at stake. For example, a good person who believes that lying is wrong would clearly concede that misdirecting some Nazi guards away from where some Jews are hiding is perfectly acceptable, even admirable. But then, some people would use the same reasoning to misdirect an independent auditor away from a flagrant accounting error. If they get away with it, they sigh a breath of relief and either begin to further rationalize the action or forget the incident entirely. Since the only person who knows what really happened is the person bending the rules (and even that's debatable), there's usually none the wiser. So I say fight fire with fire. Do what works. If you can't dialogue with evil, then you must destroy it."

"I don't think evil can be destroyed, Kevin." Kim was usually hesitant to cross Kevin in the classroom discussions, but now seemed the appropriate time. "If we fail in our attempts to heal evil, then we can only contain it."

As usual, the conversation was lively, although people seemed to be more sensitive to one another this evening, even Kevin. When it was obvious that the discussion was winding down, Jacob wrapped things up.

"Again, I appreciate all of you making it tonight. Usually our off-site meetings are a little more relaxed, but obviously that couldn't be helped in light of what happened. Wow, there's nothing like real life to put certain truths to the test, now is there? OK then, we'll see you next week."

That night, Cathy wrote in her notebook, *How much has to happen before we say, "Enough is enough"? What's going to happen when God reaches that point?*

MAKE EVERY EFFORT TO ADD TO YOUR ... KNOWLEDGE, SELF-CONTROL.

2 PETER 1:5–6

Chapter 8

Self-Control:
The Ability to Internalize Responsibility

SELF-CONTROL: 1. Control of one's emotions, desires, or actions by one's own will. 2. To exercise authoritative or dominating influence over. 3. To adjust to a requirement; regulate. 4. To hold in restraint; check. 5. To reduce or prevent the spread of something. 6. Authority or ability to manage or direct.

YourDictionary.com

*I*n our sinful state, it's easy to confuse being made in the image of God with being God.

Having the image of God in us means that we are finite representations of God's attributes. God is all-powerful; we have some power. God is all-knowing; we have some knowledge. God is omnipresent, that is, he exists in his totality at every point in space. As human beings, we can only exist in one place at one time. God controls everything; God instructs us to exercise to self-control.

That last one is a tall order.

Self-control usually has connotations of "keeping a tight rein" on sinful thoughts and desires. And that is certainly right and true. It's also true that people often fall short in this area because of the weakness of the human will.

A few of these folks who keep trying and trying sometimes sink into a deep despair, wanting to change but not really knowing how. These folks are in the best of all possible positions for change, for they have finally reached the point of saying that they don't have the power within themselves to do everything that is needed. How they deal with this acknowledgment makes all the difference.

In full recognition of the thousands and thousands of people who have been helped by twelve-step programs, I respectfully take exception to the premise behind Step 1: "We admitted we were powerless over [blank] and that our lives had become unmanageable."[1]

If the Bible calls us to self-control (as we see in 2 Peter 1:5–6), then self-control is possible. One cannot be *permanently* powerless and still exercise any degree of self-control. If I am truly powerless, then I cannot be held morally responsible for my actions. As convenient as it might be to believe that, it's simply never going to be consistent with reality—for me or for anyone else.

With rare exceptions, powerlessness is always temporary, and the goal of self-control is to do whatever it takes to get whatever help it takes to move from that transitory state to one of personal responsibility and empowerment.

There's really a simple key to accomplishing this.

The essence of self-control is dependent on what counselors call the "locus of control." *Locus* is defined as "a center or focus of great activity or intense concentration."[2] Our ability to control our feelings, thoughts, words, attitudes, and actions depends on where that locus is.

If it's outside of ourselves, that is, if our locus of control rests with other people and circumstances, then our ability to take responsibility for our actions (and to avoid repeating the same mistakes) is diminished significantly. If the locus of control is within us, that is, if we rightly believe that we have 100 percent control over how we *respond* to people, circumstances, and temptation, then self-control is not only going to exist, but also become stronger as time goes on.

One of the tests of happiness, in my opinion, is knowing the difference between what we can control, what we can merely influence, and what is completely outside the range of our effective will. The differences can be clarified as follows:

What we can control: what we initiate and our response to life's circumstances.
What we can only influence: what others initiate and how they respond to life's circumstances.
What is outside the range of our effective will: everything else.

That phrase "the range of effective will" was coined by Dr. Dallas Willard, not only to define the kingdom of God ("the range of God's effective will"), but also to help us understand our own "minikingdoms."[3]

Your Own Personal Kingdom

Dr. Willard has an interesting question that he likes to pose to Christians and non-Christians alike. He asks, "How is your kingdom doing today?" Regardless of their answer, they must give pause to the credibility of the question.[4] They must ask themselves, *Do I even have a kingdom? And if I do, how's it going?*

According to Willard, the kingdom of each individual is the range of his or her effective will. In a sense, every human being represents a minicivilization having an economy, a degree of health, transportation, defense, etc. A person's dominion, that is, the range of his or her effective will, varies widely among human beings.[5]

The range of the effective will of a stay-at-home mom may be "limited" to her husband, her children, and her social circle. The CEO of a Fortune 500 company may also have a family, as well as the burden of the livelihoods of thousands of people to sustain. The latter's *influence* may be greater, but the range of the mom's effective will may be significantly larger. So her "kingdom" will have bigger impact both in this age and in the age to come. Again, it all depends on how much God trusts either the mom or the CEO.

If we accept the idea that we are all in our own little kingdoms, we have to eventually decide if we are going to perpetuate our little kingdoms with the hopes that they will endure or if we will voluntarily subject our little kingdoms to the kingdom of God, offering up all of the resources of our minikingdoms for the advancement of God's dominion.

On the surface, the decision seems easy. Of course, why wouldn't I do such a thing? God is so much bigger than I. Of course I will surrender. But how often, from a practical standpoint, does this happen? Most people think that they can devote their lives to building their own kingdoms and then, when they die, simply enter heaven.

Nothing could be further from the truth.

The Bible is one of those books that makes you want to read the ending to see how everything concludes. At the end of the Bible we read this:

> There were great voices in heaven, saying, The kingdoms of this world are become the kingdoms of our Lord, and of his Christ; and he shall reign for ever and ever. (Rev. 11:15 KJV)

All the kingdoms of men and women, rulers, powers, and authorities in the heavenly realms are eventually going to be absorbed into the kingdom of God. The only question is whether they do so voluntarily or eventually against their will.

This is why Jesus admonished us to "seek the [advancement of the] kingdom of God first, then all these things [that is, the security

> Many people not only lose the benefit, but are even the worse for their mortifications [i.e., sacrifices, abstensions] ... because they mistake the whole nature and worth of them: they practice them for their own sakes, as things good in themselves, they think them to be real parts of holiness, so rest in them and look no further, but grow full of a self-esteem and self-admiration for their own progress in them. This makes them self-sufficient, morose, severe judges of all those that fall short of their mortifications. And thus their self-denials do only that for them which indulgences do for other people: they withstand and hinder the operation of God upon their souls, and instead of being really self-denials, they strengthen and keep up the kingdom of self.
> —WILLIAM LAW (1686–1761), *The Spirit of Prayer* (1749)

which we believe our minikingdoms will provide] will be added unto us" (see Matt. 6:33).

Ruling under Authority

There is a good reason that self-control follows knowledge in Peter's list of traits. (Again, self-control is something that he wants us to add to our knowledge.) As our "knowledge of the secrets of the kingdom" (Matt. 13:11) grows, so will the depth of our response (the only thing we can control) to that knowledge.

Submitting our minikingdoms to God's kingdom (in many and varied ways we can do that) *does not mean* that we lose or give up control. I believe that was the error of the man who buried his talent, thinking that the master was so powerful that he would take care of everything anyway. And we all remember how the master responded to that type of faulty thinking.

Self-control, when it comes to submitting to God, simply means that we respond (the only thing we can control) to God in a way that honors him—namely, by internalizing responsibility for our thoughts, words, and actions. And if those thoughts, words, and actions bear fruit, we should offer those resources to God. And if those thoughts, words, and actions end up dishonoring God, then we acknowledge the blame and take whatever midcourse corrections are necessary. Failing in that, we ask for mercy.

The person whom God trusts is able to consistently internalize responsibility for his or her thoughts, words, and actions.

MAKE EVERY EFFORT TO ADD TO YOUR ... SELF-CONTROL, PERSEVERANCE.

2 PETER 1:5–6

CHAPTER 9

PERSEVERANCE:
Dealing with Loss in the Best of All Possible Worlds

PERSEVERANCE: 1. STEADY PERSISTENCE IN ADHERING TO A COURSE OF ACTION, A BELIEF, OR A PURPOSE; STEADFASTNESS. 2. THE CALVINISTIC DOCTRINE THAT THOSE WHO HAVE BEEN CHOSEN BY GOD WILL CONTINUE IN A STATE OF GRACE TO THE END AND WILL FINALLY BE SAVED.

MERRIAM-WEBSTER DICTIONARY

I WAS RAISED BY TWO SICK PEOPLE WHO TAUGHT ME INSANITY AND FEAR AND HATRED. I WAS RAISED IN HELL, AND CHAOS FELT LIKE HOME. RESULT: I LEARNED TO LAND ON MY FEET IN ANY SITUATION, AND I CAN STAND FACE-TO-FACE WITH THE CRUELEST OF OGRES.
STEVEN J. WOLIN, *THE RESILIENT SELF*

We live in the best of all possible worlds.

How you respond to that statement depends in large part on the types of losses you've experienced in life, either due to tragedy, personal failure, or the negligence or malice of others.

Some who have led relatively peaceful lives may respond by saying, "Sure, that's conceivable. The world has some problems, but for the most part, we're learning to overcome them."

For some people who have been severely traumatized, however, such a statement might be greeted with anger, bitterness, and no small degree of skepticism.

In fact, when the great tsunami of 2004 hit the shorelines of Southeast Asia, taking tens of thousands of lives, there was a lot of chatter in the media and on the Internet around the question "How could God allow this to happen?"

It's a fair question.

The problem of evil (natural and moral) has perplexed philosophers and theologians alike for centuries. In a nutshell, this problem has been defined like this: We cannot claim that God is all-powerful and completely good if evil exists.

So the argument goes: God is either good but not all-powerful (he wants to eliminate evil but can't), or God is all-powerful but not completely good (he has the power to eliminate evil but doesn't care enough to get the job done). Or God is neither all-good nor all-powerful, which makes him not much different from the deities in Greek mythology.

But if we are to believe the Scriptures, then all three things obviously are true: God is omnipotent, omnibenevolent, and the heavens and the earth are filled with people and angelic beings who are utterly bent on the exploitation, domination, and destruction of others.

So how do we resolve this paradox?

One seventeenth-century philosopher (better known for his work in mathematics) who attempted to tackle the problem was Gottfried Leibniz. Leibniz assumed that if God, being loving, benevolent, and all-powerful, was going to create a world, he'd create the best of all possible worlds. Why would he create anything less? So Leibniz concluded, the best of all possible worlds includes the existence of evil. The only way for evil to exist is for it to be freely chosen.[1]

So, in a nutshell, the best of all possible worlds insists on being populated with created beings who have the ability to freely choose good or evil, decisions for which they can legitimately be held morally responsible.

C. S. Lewis builds upon this principle to help us understand how this could even be:

> Some people think they can imagine a creature which was free but had no possibility of going wrong; I cannot.... Because free will, though it makes evil possible, is also the only thing that makes possible any love or goodness or joy worth having.[2]

God, as a truly loving being, could not force human beings to love him, to become automatons. God even gave the angels the choice to stay or rebel. Once they made their choices, the consequences were eternal. Fallen angels can never be redeemed, nor will they ever desire redemption.

Therefore, the best of all possible worlds is one in which free will exists, where people can be held morally responsible for their thoughts, words, and actions.

In such a world where free will exists, human beings will voluntarily choose evil, and they must be allowed to do so for the integrity of the system to hold up. As a result, evil actions result in evil consequences, and thus sometimes innocent people suffer.

Leslie Weatherhead, in his book *The Will of God,* presents an interesting analogy to illustrate how the ultimate will of God is always accomplished. He likened it to a stream running down a hill:

> In their sinfulness and rebellion, people have tried to divert the flow of a stream, using whatever means at their disposal. No matter what kinds of dams, structures, or obstacles men might place in this path (in the abusive exercise of their free will), the water will work around it. While delayed, the water always reaches its final destination, be it a puddle, pond, lake, sea or ocean. Despite the most diabolical attempts of men to divert the stream (that is, the ultimate will of God), the water always reaches its destination.[3]

With gratitude to Mr. Weatherhead, I'd like to expand upon his analogy.

Imagine the world when it was first created as a gently sloping hill in the middle of which ran a stream of living water. When man first sinned, he stepped into the stream in an effort to divert the flow. And the stream was diverted a little. The banks suddenly started to get a little muddy, and it got to be a little harder to walk about the hill. But the water was relentless in the pursuit of its destination.

> *The fear of loss is the path to the dark side.*
>
> —YODA, JEDI MASTER IN THE FILM STAR WARS, EPISODE III

As man's rebellion grew, he became more and more bent upon diverting the stream, so he started throwing twigs and branches into it. Of course, in order to do this he had to destroy a few fruit-bearing trees. No matter. The need to rebel far overwhelmed his desire to eat.

As the water continued to diverge, not only did the banks get muddier, but also the whole hillside soon became thick with mud and water. Waste started to pile up and mix in with the mud. Those who tried to make it up the hill found the way getting slow and sludgy.

Frustrated with the tenacity of the water, men started throwing boulders into the stream to further divert its flow. When they realized that they were still failing, they started killing each other and throwing the bodies in.

But, by the grace of God, people were still able to trudge up this muddy, sticky hill called Life. About two thousand years ago, God became a man and showed people by his example how to make it through the sludge. Only one or two folks have made it up the hill without dying first (and those exceptions were the gift of God).

And this, believe it or not, is what the best of all possible worlds looks like: one in which free will exists and people are held responsible for their actions. Moving toward God (as we move through life) means trudging uphill, in the sludge, with some making progress, some getting stuck, and some giving up entirely.

Salvation doesn't mean getting plucked up from the sludge and taken up to the top, though some believe that they are entitled to such a rescue. It simply means that Jesus trudges up the hill with us.

When Jesus confronted Saul on the way to Damascus, he asked, "Why are you persecuting Me?" (Acts 9:4 NASB). How could that be if Jesus was standing at the right hand of God in heaven? It's true because Jesus is no mere observer to our pain and suffering, but an active participant within in it.

Therein, somewhere, lies an answer to the mystery posed by the problem of evil: that God suffers along with us.

> *The army's disposition of force is like water. Just as water's configuration avoids heights and races downward, so the army's disposition of force avoids the substantial and strikes the vacuous. Water configures its flow in accord with the terrain: the army controls its victory in accord with the enemy.*
>
> —SUN TZU, THE ART OF WAR

In regard to coping with the consequences of free will, let's expand another analogy, one offered by C. S. Lewis. Two groups of people are taken to a mediocre resort, where the sheets *might* be clean and you'd be lucky if the vending machines work.

The first group is told that they're heading toward a five-star hotel and to expect the best of what that luxury has to afford. The second group is told they're being taken to a concentration camp and should not expect to survive the year.

When the people arrive, the first group is aghast at what they discover and therefore complain loudly because reality is not meeting up to their expectations. The second group arrives expecting deprivation and is pleasantly surprised to discover that the accommodations are really not that bad.[4]

So it is walking up the sludgy hill of life in the best of all possible worlds. In the Advancing Dominion, that is the actual condition the world is in, and we should not expect it to be any other way. Those who are expecting it to be different, who are consumed with a sense of entitlement, spend most of their days emotionally miserable and increasingly embittered.

This is an opportunity-rich environment in which to build upon the trust we already have with God.

> Then [Paul and Barnabas] returned to Lystra, Iconium and Antioch, strengthening the disciples and encouraging them to remain true to the faith. "We must go through many hardships to enter the kingdom of God," they said. (Acts 14:21–22)

Let's explore this further.

THE BLESSING OF LOSS

After a string of crushing losses that ended with the death of my first child shortly after he was born, my prayers to God had been reduced to a four-word question: *Do you love me?*

Jesus asked this question of Peter, so I figured there must be some context in which this question was legitimate. It's easy to feel in times of loss that we have somehow lost the love of God. We think, *How could God love me if this happened to me? Couldn't he have prevented it? And if he is all-powerful, why didn't he? Unless, of course, he doesn't love me as much, perhaps, as I thought.*

The Lord answered my question with two other questions: Are there people in the Bible who experienced significant loss? If so, did my love for them diminish in any way?

To answer the first question, I searched the Scriptures and found a multitude of stories about personal loss: some due to circumstances beyond the control of the Bible character and some due to his or her own negligence or even sin. Among those I discovered were the following:

- Adam and Eve lost the garden, and one of their sons was murdered.
- Moses was not allowed to enter the Promised Land that he had waited for more than forty years to see.
- Samson lost his eyesight.
- Job lost his livelihood, his health, his wife's respect, and all of his children.
- David lost his baby boy and two grown sons.
- Daniel never returned to his homeland.
- Jeremiah never had a wife.
- Ruth and Naomi lost their husbands.
- Lot and Ezekiel lost their wives.
- Hosea lost the ability to trust his wife.
- Elisha lost his friend and mentor.
- Joseph was not allowed to be at his mother's deathbed.
- James and John the Baptist were beheaded by members of the same tyrannical family.
- Paul was falsely accused and imprisoned.
- Mary was widowed and then watched her son be executed.
- Abigail endured years of emotional abuse.
- Nehemiah was falsely accused and hindered in his work.

- Jeremiah was thrown in a well and left for dead.
- Jonah lost his dignity.
- Mary and Martha lost their brother.
- Peter and Silas lost their freedom.
- Barnabas lost a friend while sticking up for another.

> Evil instinctively knows what you are unwilling to lose and will tempt you with the possibility of loss and heartbreak.... Evil will never be conquered as long as our hearts live to obtain immediate relief or escape profound loss. Only when we have little or nothing to lose will we be willing to love [the evil person].
>
> —Dan Allender, Bold Love

So I considered the lives of these people and thought, *Did God's love for these folks diminish in the least because of their losses?*

I had to say no.

And then the Lord seemed to say, "If this is true, then apply this truth to yourself."

Paul made it clear that some believers will suffer loss at heaven's door, and the type of loss will be caused by their own negligence, stubbornness, or long-standing sins. But despite this loss, God's love for them will not diminish in the least.

And this is the first blessing. Many will understand for the first time in their eternal lives what God means by unconditional love. Unconditional love does not mean the absence of loss or the withholding of discipline. But we will see, finally, that despite our losses—even those due to our own negligence—God's love for us will not diminish in the least.

Convinced of this truth, I want everything that has no genuine substance within me to be purged from my soul as soon as possible—if not in this life, then certainly at heaven's door.

Ask anyone who has had cancer, and he will likely tell you that his first thought was, *I want this out of my body as quickly as possible.* Now many folks avoid the doctor at the first suspicion of cancer because they just don't want to know about it; it's a very dangerous form of blissful ignorance, indeed. But once it's brought to their attention and they've passed entirely through the denial phase, they just want it out.

Sometimes we spend so much energy trying to prevent loss because of its strong association with not feeling loved, either by God or by others—while, in fact, the Word of God tells us to expect inevitable losses in our lives because of our association with Jesus.

> By faith Moses, when he had grown up, refused to be known as the son of Pharaoh's daughter. He chose to be mistreated along with the people of God rather than to enjoy the pleasures of sin for a short time. [Moses] regarded disgrace *for the sake of Christ* as of greater value than the treasures of Egypt, because he was looking ahead to his reward. (Heb. 11:24–26)

> Some faced jeers and flogging, while still others were chained and put in prison. They were stoned; they were sawed in two; they were put to death by the sword. They went about in sheepskins and goatskins, destitute, persecuted and mistreated. (Heb. 11:36–37)

> If anyone would come after me, he must deny himself and take up his cross daily and follow me. (Luke 9:23)

The kingdom of God is a place where obedience thrives, not merely out of a sense of duty, but as a means to move forward through our fears. When we're afraid of losing things that are dear to us, we tend to hold back. But if we entrust the actual or possible loss into God's hands as we move forward in obedience, then carrying out the will of God seems easier.

You Can Take It with You!

That's what Ron Luce, in his book *Battle Cry for a Generation*, tells us is so effective about the military. When you enlist, you take an oath to follow all lawful orders, even if it means laying one's life on the line, which is the ultimate sacrifice, and yet we move forward anyway.[6]

If there's some cancerous attitude within me, some lingering bitterness or well-hidden pride, then I want the deception to be removed as quickly as possible. As C. S. Lewis once implied if the sum and substance of a person's faith is little more than a house of cards, the sooner it falls the better.[5]

MAKE EVERY EFFORT TO ADD TO YOUR ... PERSEVERANCE, GODLINESS.

2 PETER 1:5-6

Chapter 10

Godliness:
Imitating God

GODLINESS: 1. THE STATE OF BEING GODLY.

GODLY 1. HAVING GREAT REVERENCE FOR GOD. 2. THE WHOLE OF PRACTICAL PIETY (SEE 1 TIM. 4:8; 2 PETER 1:6). IT SUPPOSES KNOWLEDGE, VENERATION, AFFECTION, DEPENDENCE, SUBMISSION, GRATITUDE, AND OBEDIENCE. IN 1 TIMOTHY 3:16 IT DENOTES THE SUBSTANCE OF REVEALED RELIGION.

Eastern Bible Dictionary

A friend of mine who is a pastor just doesn't like to see Jesus portrayed in films. To him, there's something odd about a sinful human being (who may be very talented as an actor) portraying God Incarnate. To him, it seems that no one would really be up to the task. As far as he's concerned, we're better off imitating devils.

Therein lies the danger of defining godliness in terms of human behavior, no matter how moral or upright that behavior might be. Some Christian traditions solve this problem by portraying God in light of what he is *not*: God is not selfish, politically motivated, malicious, etc.

So perhaps the best starting point for exploring the topic of godliness is by defining the ways that we are *different* from Jesus.

Here's how it would apply in my case: God does not worry about the future or the possible losses that may lie ahead; God is not irritable with people who keep making the same mistakes; God does not hesitate to internalize responsibility for his thoughts, words, and actions.

If I start in this place, then I can more accurately answer the question "What would Jesus do?" In most cases, he would do exactly the opposite of whatever my first impulses happen to be.

I suppose the strict definition of godliness is "to be *like God.*" The whole concept of imitating God would seem humanly impossible if, in fact, it wasn't a biblical mandate: "Be imitators of God, therefore, as dearly loved children" (Eph. 5:1).

In the next few pages, we'll be speaking of godliness in terms of "sensitivity," with the first step, of course, being sensitive to the degrees to which we are different from God. Next, we'll explore being sensitive to hearing the voice of God, so we know how to best imitate him in situations that may have no clear-cut path. And, finally, we end by talking about sensitive to spiritual readiness—not only in our souls, but also others' hearts.

HEARING THE VOICE OF GOD

Sometimes it's fun to watch the moms who are hanging out in the fast-food restaurants' playland areas with their children. Quite often, you can tell how many kids they are watching at the time by the size of the stack of napkins at their tables.

Some of these moms are alone at their tables, nibbling on fries, writing in a journal, reading a book, or tapping something into their organizers. Many of them have a relaxed look on their faces because they're finally getting a break while the kids play in a "contained area"—unless, of course, one of the kids thinks it would be fun to escape through an emergency exit and set off an alarm.

Some of the moms are there chatting with friends, occasionally looking up to see one of their kids tapping from the inside of a Plexiglas bubble, trying to get their attention. Again, whether these moms are alone or with a friend, most of them seem to be at ease and enjoying themselves.

But then, suddenly, some kid starts crying, and all the moms stop what they're doing to pay attention. When this happens, each one of the moms asks herself two questions: "Is that *my kid* crying?" and "Is it the type of crying that's worthy of my attention?"

Sometimes kids let out bloodcurdling screams because they've been injured and need immediate attention. Other times kids cry because their feelings have been hurt or they've been denied access to a particular tube—nothing that an ice-cream cone won't fix—and then they're back having fun.

These scenes reflect a natural axiom of the universe that's as unchangeable as the law of gravity: Loving moms *know* their kids' voices and how to react appropriately when they hear their kids call out. It doesn't matter how many other kids are screaming at the top of their lungs in the same area; if her kid is crying, a caring mom will know it immediately and within seconds know what's necessary to rectify the situation.

Jesus understood the power of this type of "voice recognition." In his teaching that's recorded in John 10:1–10, Jesus crafted an analogy around this concept to help us better understand how we can "pick him out in a crowd of voices," regardless of the cacophony of distractions around us. If we want to be godly, if we want to be like Jesus, then we must be able to discern his voice.

Jesus began this analogy with these words: "I tell you the truth, the man who does not enter the sheep pen by the gate, but climbs in by some other way, is a thief and a robber. The man who enters by the gate is the shepherd of his sheep" (vv. 1–2).

Jesus continued to build on the contrast between the robber and the shepherd throughout this passage. The sheep listen to the voice of the shepherd because they recognize it but run away from the stranger because they are not familiar with his sound. There's something about the stranger's voice that makes the animals uneasy.

The stranger of whom Jesus spoke is not a nice guy. Jesus used words like *thief, robber, killer,* and *destroyer* to describe him. Consider the attacks on the teachers and students of Columbine High School and the bombing of the federal building in Oklahoma City. Surely the angry young men who brought this evil upon their innocent victims give us a picture of the horrible intentions of those who "[climb] in by some other way."

In contrast, Jesus tells us that the shepherd is there to protect, nurture, and provide. He is not like the hired hand who takes off as soon as trouble appears. If a lion, bear, or wolf appears on the scene, the shepherd is ready to lay down his life for the flock.

Quite often after Jesus offered a parable or a metaphor to explain a certain concept, the disciples wouldn't have a clue as to what he was talking about. Their confusion appeared again after this story, so Jesus made it plain for them. He told them what each person or entity in the analogy represented.

Surprisingly, Jesus did not identify himself as the shepherd in this word picture, but rather as the "gate." However, if you've even seen a stone sheep pen like the kind that was commonly used in the first century, you would be able to see how Jesus could be both the gate and shepherd.

Shepherds commonly let their sheep graze during the day. But, like modern-day kids, the sheep were prone to wander, especially when they might not be able to see the other sheep or their familiar shepherd. So the herder would create large circular pens for the sheep made out of the many small boulders available in the Holy Land.

After completing most of the stone circle, the shepherd would leave a five- or six-foot opening in the circle for the sheep to come in and out. (The walls were usually three or four feet high.) At night, the shepherd would sleep across the opening, using his body as a type of "gate." If any sheep tried to get out by walking over him, he would wake up and shoo them back. And if any wolf tried to get to the flock via this opening, the sleeping shepherd would be the first to know and summarily take care of the problem.

That's why the robbers, thieves, and destroyers have to "[climb] in by some other way," so as to avoid the protective attention of the shepherd. And as Jesus pointed out so poetically, the sheep only pay attention to the voice of their shepherd, not that of those who break in uninvited.

Sometimes dealing with the noise that life creates is like walking into a room with fifty radios blaring. We need to be able to shut out all that noise and tune in to the whisper that the prophet Isaiah described: "Whether you turn to the right or to the left, your ears will hear a voice behind you, saying, 'This is the way; walk in it'" (30:21).

So how do we hear and recognize the voice of God?

First, we must immerse ourselves in the Scriptures, for they are made up entirely of the voice of God. Nothing that the Lord says to us in any other context will contradict what the Bible says. Those who come to "steal and ... destroy," however, will always echo the doubt-generating words of the Serpent in the garden: "Did God really say that?" If the Word of God permeates our thinking, we'll have a better idea of what God has to say to us in almost any situation.

The second thing we do is turn off all the "radios." If fifty of them are blaring at us all at once, we need to simply remove ourselves from within earshot, if even for just a few moments. Listen to the testimony of one woman who was able to get away so she could listen:

You Can Take It with You!

Once, after a particularly claustrophobic, stressful, and overpopulated time when there hadn't been air or space to escape to, suddenly, for a few days, I was alone. It was like emigrating to another planet (while in fact, I was at home). Who was this person I was living with, this stranger, this reasonable, serene foreigner in the house; a becalmed woman who spent her time inwardly humming?[1]

Solitude and silence are wonderful amphitheaters in which to hear the symphony of God's voice. If you're facing a particularly difficult situation, perhaps you need to just carve out a time of retreat so that you can hear from the Lord. Just get away from the hustle and bustle of everyday life. Don't try to think too hard; just sit and be still. Prayers of silence are not only for the mystics, you know.

Of course, all of us have heard from well-meaning people who claim that the Lord has spoken to them directly concerning a particular matter, so they are unwavering in their resolve to complete the divine mandate. As we roll our eyes, we may wonder, "So how do I know if I've really heard from the Lord or if I'm just talking to myself, putting a divine stamp on something I just came up with on my own?"

In a spirit of humility, we should bring all of our "impressions from the Lord" to mature and trusted believers to get their discerning input. In fact, the Lord may even continue to speak through them to us.

If our thinking is guided by Scripture and our prayers are marked by a sense of receptivity, we will hear and recognize the voice of God. And as we bring these messages to those we trust for confirmation and affirmation, we can be assured that the loving and guiding voice of the Holy Spirit is directing our paths.

Let us plan times of solitude and reflection to focus our attention on what the Spirit of God may want to whisper to our souls, for this is the essence of godliness.

SENSING SPIRITUAL READINESS

As many people know, the Jews walked around Samaria on their way to and from Jerusalem, even though it added a full day to their journey. The Samaritans were the descendants of Jews and their foreign spouses who were left in the homeland during the exile. So they were considered by many of the Jews to be "unclean." To distinguish themselves from their Jewish cousins, the Samaritans set up a temple in Samaria and considered only the Pentateuch as canonical. In addition to these bothersome characteristics, the Samaritans were also a constant reminder of the preexilic Jews' failure to honor, serve, and obey God, which had resulted in them being expelled from the land.

In the midst of this acrimonious tension, Jesus walked right into Samaria, delegated some grocery shopping to the disciples, and asked a Samaritan woman for a drink of water. Scandalous. There was a tradition of separatist purity that Jesus seemed to be ignoring, and the woman wasted no time pointing this out to the Lord.

Always the opportunist (in the best possible sense), Jesus used the woman's surprising reaction as a bridge to the gospel. "Jesus answered her, 'If you knew the gift of God and who it is that asks you for a drink, you would have asked him and he would have given you living water'" (John 4:10).

Note the emphasis that Jesus placed on asking.

Few people realize this, but the woman could have ignored the setup, politely given Jesus his drink of water, and walked away. Or she could have smiled, nodded her head, and just changed the subject.

Instead of ignoring the statement, however, the woman chose to keep the conversation going by asking Jesus how he was going to get this water if, in fact, he had nothing with which to draw it.

In response to her legitimate question, Jesus took his analogy to the next level and stated that the water of which he spoke is living and utterly satisfying to the one who partakes. With this statement he gave her yet another chance to either respond or politely bring the conversation to a close.

With her curiosity aroused, she asked Jesus for some of this "miracle water" so she would not have to keep coming to this place in the heat of the day just to survive. Instead of clarifying what he meant, however, Jesus took a sudden left turn in the conversation and asked her to go get her husband.

Gulp! Water was a much easier subject.

Husband was not a friendly word for this woman. As we find out later, she had been married and probably divorced five times, and she was currently sleeping with a man to whom she was not married. This woman was about to be put on the spot, and she knew it. So she gave a response that was technically true ("I have no husband" [John 4:17]), but she intended to misrepresent her actual situation.

Jesus lovingly called her on it and prophetically described her exact station in life. Now that Jesus had gone from "preachin'" to "meddlin'," she attempted to change the subject by focusing on her ancestors' religious history and traditions. She might as well have been talking about the weather, because the last thing she wanted exposed any further was her long string of tragic and painful marital failures.

So Jesus compassionately allowed the diversion, without losing his focus on the gift of God's grace that he longed for this woman to accept. With hope building within her, she brought up God's promise to send a Messiah. In one of the few places in all of the Gospels, Jesus directly identified himself as that prophesied Savior.

At this point the woman left the well and her valuable water jar. But she was not taking off because of awkwardness or discomfort. A spiritual light had come on for her, for she had finally understood and accepted the grace of God for the first time in her life, and she needed to tell somebody.

The lessons we can learn from this spirited conversation can be seen in Jesus' admonition to the disciples and the woman's actions after she left the well. Jesus told his disciples to stop waiting around for opportunities to share the gospel and to go out and start creating them, as he had just done. They should do this while still, of course, giving the lost the opportunity to back out of the conversation if in fact the Holy Spirit had not prepared their hearts to receive God's truth. Many believers who have graciously not extended an unsolicited spiritual conversation often find themselves picking it up where they left off. Over the course of time, a seeker often moves into a state of spiritual readiness that he or she was not in previously.

The woman at the well had certainly learned the lesson of effective evangelism. John wrote, "Many of the Samaritans from that town believed in him because of the woman's testimony" (4:39).

And her testimony was simply this: "He told me everything I did" (see v. 29). What a contrast in this woman's attitude about her past! Before, she was ducking any conversation about her own sinfulness. Now she had freely acknowledged her sinful past. Since she had been the grateful recipient of God's grace, she could talk about her tragic life in a matter-of-fact manner. What she had done and who knew about it no longer mattered to her. She simply told the story about what Jesus had done for her and then asked her own open-ended question: "Could this be the Christ?"

After spending a few days with Jesus, many more of the townsfolk came to believe in him. Then the passage ends with a curious statement from the crowds to the woman. Their words to her were courteous but blunt. They wanted to make it clear that they no longer believed solely on the basis of her testimony but because they had experienced Jesus for themselves.

I'm sure the woman at the well smiled inwardly when she heard these words. She didn't want them to live out her particular faith experience but rather to "own" what they believed so they could live it out in the unique ways that God had prepared for them.

And this should be our goal as well as we seek to reach the lost. Let us not be ashamed of what we've been saved from. If we've acknowledged our sin, then it doesn't matter what we've done or who knows about it. In fact, if shared appropriately, this type of vulnerability might be the very thing that compels folks to consider Christ's claims for themselves.

In addition, as Michael Simpson reminds us in *Permission Evanglism,* let's not hesitate to walk away from a spiritual conversation if our friend is clearly not ready to receive God's truth. Keep the door open, and if the Spirit so chooses, you'll be able to pick things up later where you left them off.

And finally, be prepared for people to have very different salvation experiences from your own. There are as many conversion stories as there are personalities, so we must share the gospel in such a way that it allows our friends to experience Jesus for themselves.

MAKE EVERY EFFORT TO ADD TO YOUR ... GODLINESS, BROTHERLY KINDNESS.

2 PETER 1:5, 7

KINGDOM SPOTLIGHT

TRAINING TO REIGN

God certainly understands the concept of human development, that we're not able to simply "get it all at once." While instant knowledge and ability make for good science fiction, we seem to be somewhat limited in how fast, and how well, we can take it in.

Several Scriptures seem to imply that God expects us to go through training—the type of training for skills needed not only in this life, but also in the life to come. As Dallas Willard has said, we are "training to reign."[2]

> Praise be to the LORD my Rock, who trains my hands for war, my fingers for battle. (Ps. 144:1)

> I trained them and strengthened them, but they plot evil against me. (Hos. 7:15)

> Everyone who competes in the games goes into strict training. (1 Cor. 9:25)

> A student is not above his teacher, but everyone who is fully trained will be like his teacher. (Luke 6:40)

> Blessed and holy are those who have part in the first resurrection. The second death has no power over them, but they will be priests of God and of Christ and will reign with him for a thousand years. (Rev. 20:6)

So, in a sense, life is a dress rehearsal.

CHAPTER 11

KINDNESS:
The Power of Empathy

KINDNESS: 1. The state of being kind.

KIND: 1. Of a friendly, generous, or warm-hearted nature. 2. Showing sympathy or understanding; charitable. 3. Humane; considerate. 4. Forbearing; tolerant. 5. Generous. 6. Agreeable.

Synonyms: kind, kindly, kindhearted, benign, benevolent. *Kindhearted* especially suggests an innately kind disposition. *Benign* implies gentleness and mildness. *Benevolent* suggests charitableness and a desire to promote the welfare or happiness of others.

Dictionary.com

*L*innie was a bag lady. After spending forty-two years in a state mental hospital, she was released to the world to make it on her own. One day an older gentleman named Elton discovered her rummaging through his garbage, looking for something to eat. As respectfully as he could, he asked Linnie, "Would you like some hot soup?" Her face, marred by years of distrust and misgivings, relaxed a little at the prospect of some hot food in her stomach. So without a saying a word, she accepted Elton's invitation and came into his kitchen, where his wife offered Linnie something warm to eat.

Every day at the same time for the next six months, Linnie arrived at Elton's doorstep, and she was welcomed in for some hot soup. During this entire time, she did not say a single word.

Finally, one morning after Linnie was finished eating, she said, "My name is Linnie Pierce. Thank you for the soup."

As Linnie's ability to trust grew, Elton was able to find additional help for her, including medical attention, legal representation, and a safe place to live.

Hal Haralson, who tells Linnie's story in his book *Gentle Mercies*, states that when Linnie died at the age of ninety, it was discovered that she had over $100,000 in personal assets, money she had accumulated over the years by selling pecans that she had collected in a Styrofoam cup.[1]

A Genuine Heart to Love

Elton's compassion for Linnie and his willingness to give without compensation serve well as an introduction to the passage in Matthew 9—10. Matthew tells us that when Jesus came upon a large gathering of people, "he had compassion on them, because they were harassed and helpless, like sheep without a shepherd" (9:36). This was the relational, unapologetically emotional base from which Jesus conducted every aspect of his ministry: his miracles, his teaching, his healings, and ultimately, even his death on the cross. The apostles Paul and Peter made it clear that we are to follow Jesus' example in all things (see 1 Cor. 11:1; 1 Peter 2:21), and imitating the Lord's compassion for others, especially those who are hurting and seem lost, is certainly a good place to start.

Out of this genuine sense of kindness and compassion, Jesus told his followers to ask the Lord of the harvest (God) to send more workers out into the field of ministry because the "harvest" was bountiful.

We can see two assumptions from this teaching. First, Jesus was addressing those who were *already* in the field, bringing in the harvest. Our request is not to be sent, but to ask for more help. Second, since the harvest was plentiful and ready to be collected, we can assume that the people Jesus was describing were (and are) not only ready to hear and receive the good news of the kingdom, but also they were (and are) chomping at the bit to get out there and bear fruit for God.

Often, when we're planning to "do" evangelism, we feel the need to get psyched up for rejection. We assume that the people on our "target list" are going to be hostile, not only to us, but also to the claims of Christ. Let me assure you that as soon as someone figures our that he or she is your evangelism "project," you should expect an aggressive response, and perhaps deservedly so. Most people can tell when an evangelist is disingenuous—even when they're hurting and possibly looking for some spiritual direction.

In contrast, when we follow the example of Jesus and approach the lost with a heart of compassion, all fear of rejection disappears. Compassion will drive us to find out about the person, his likes, dislikes, and possible spiritual needs. If he's clearly not ready to hear the gospel, if the Holy Spirit has not brought him to that point, then any sort of "harvest" would clearly be premature, so the God-honoring thing to do is to politely walk away from spiritual aspects of your conversations and wait on the Lord. You'll be surprised at how many times the person whose degree of spiritual readiness you respected will later (sometimes months or years later) pick up the conversation where you left it.

When Jesus called his twelve disciples (who are named in this passage), he "gave them authority to drive out evil spirits and to heal every disease and sickness" (Matt. 10:1). Volumes have been written about whether or not believers have this type of miraculous power available to them today. There are some who propose that only the apostles were given this power in order to authoritatively establish themselves in a Middle Eastern culture where this show of

KINGDOM SPOTLIGHT

WHO GETS THE KINGDOM?

As we've discussed, there are many different Christian views about what heavenly rewards are based upon. (Clearly, this is one of the "nonessentials" of the faith where there should be significant freedom of discussion among believers.) Most of these views use certain biblical passages as their basis.

The kingdom will be given to those with childlike faith.

> Jesus said, "Let the little children come to me, and do not hinder them, for the kingdom of heaven belongs to such as these." (Matt. 19:14)

The kingdom will be given to those who are humble.

> Blessed are the poor in spirit, for theirs is the kingdom of heaven. (Matt. 5:3)

The kingdom will be given to those who are maliciously persecuted for their faith.

> Blessed are those who are persecuted because of righteousness, for theirs is the kingdom of heaven. (Matt. 5:10)

The kingdom will be given to those who exercise their power without abusing it.

> Blessed are the meek, for they will inherit the earth. (Matt. 5:5)

The kingdom will simply be given to those whom God trusts.

> "Well done, my good servant!" his master replied. "Because you have been trustworthy in a very small matter, take charge of ten cities." (Luke 19:17)

The kingdom will simply be given to those to whom God is pleased to give it.

> I will give you the keys of the kingdom of heaven; whatever you bind on earth will be bound in heaven, and whatever you loose on earth will be loosed in heaven. (Matt. 16:19)

> Do not be afraid, little flock, for your Father has been pleased to give you the kingdom. (Luke 12:32)

power was essential for establishing credibility. Of course, there are many believers today, especially in second- and third-world countries, who claim that this kind of miraculous deliverance is an everyday occurrence.

This we know for sure: Jesus Christ has given us permission to proclaim the gospel with compassionate power and authority, whether or not that proclamation is accompanied by miracles. Many of the Old Testament prophets were given spectacular signs and visions—except for Jeremiah, who was only given object lessons to present. No wonder he was called the "Weeping Prophet." But was his message any less powerful? We'd have to say no.

And would anyone deny that, to some extent, Linnie had been delivered from at least some of her demons by Elton's compassion? Again, we'd have to say no.

There is no more powerful demon-expelling, spiritually healing, miraculous force in the universe than genuine, Christ-centered kindness and compassion.

After empowering his disciples to go out and preach the gospel, and after providing a compassionate example for them to follow, Jesus gave them some unusual instructions:

> Do not go among the Gentiles or enter any town of the Samaritans. Go rather to the lost sheep of Israel. As you go, preach this message: "The kingdom of heaven is near." Heal the sick, raise the dead, cleanse those who have leprosy, drive out demons. (Matt. 10:5–8)

The time would come when the apostles would take the good news of the kingdom to the Gentiles. Peter brought the good news to Cornelius, a centurion in what was known as the Italian Regiment. Of course, the apostle Paul brought the gospel to Macedonia and Rome. Tradition tells us that Thomas took the message of God's peace and reconciliation to India. The time for taking

RESCUED BY KINDNESS

Some good friends of the family, after attempting to adopt a baby from Romania, found that the doors were closing. They already had five children, which excluded them from adopting from other countries, namely China. Finally, after months and months of waiting, a door opened in Russia.

After all the arrangements were made, the mom was able to finally meet her new baby. When she did, she knew right away that this was God's child for her. She packed all of the baby's things from the orphanage and knew the last hoop to jump through was appearing before a Russian judge.

When the mom appeared before the judge, she was asked, point blank, "How can you love someone else's child when you already have five of your own?" To which the mom replied, "The heart has an infinite capacity to love." Smiling, the judge signed the papers, and the new family member was on his way home.

---

the good news to the Gentiles was coming. But for this mission, Jesus wanted his disciples to focus on a particular group, namely, their peers, the lost sheep of Israel.

A Focused Ministry

Sometimes the prospect of ministry can seem overwhelming. There are so many needs, so many people asking for help. Sometimes people joke about "saving the world," but there are a few of us who actually believe that we're capable of doing it, and we burn out in the process.

In Matthew 10, we see Jesus telling his disciples to focus their ministry on a particular group, not to spread themselves too thin. The prospect of withholding the gospel from a particular people group, even for a short period of time, seems to go against the grain of our desire to bring the gospel to the world. Regardless of our ministry ambitions, however, God wants us to focus where we are, starting with the smallest group possible (like our families and peers) and then perhaps to branch out. Paul asked Timothy a difficult rhetorical question when it came to choosing church leaders: "If anyone does not know how to manage his own family, how can he take care of God's church?" (1 Tim. 3:5). Our ministry priorities must begin at home before we even start thinking of expanding the sphere of our influence.

Jesus ended this particular teaching with these words: "Freely you have received, freely give" (Matt. 10:8). Consider the story of Elton and Linnie. Elton had freely received the grace of God; he had seen the Lord work many times in his own life, even when things seemed dire. And when he saw one of the Lord's lost sheep, he had compassion on her and invited her in to be with his family, to partake in the abundance that God had provided for him.

This is the attitude that Jesus wants us to adopt in all our ministry, not a ministry motivated a begrudging sense of duty or obligation, but a free and generous spirit, one that is grateful for what's been given and energized by passing along some of those gifts.

Let's keep these encouraging words in mind: "Freely you have received, freely give" (Matt. 10:8). Take an inventory of what God has provided for you. Show kindness and compassion to those who may have experienced a recent loss or seem to be in need of direction. With genuine compassion and with sensitivity to their spiritual readiness, let us always be ready to give a reason for the hope that abides within us.

MAKE EVERY EFFORT TO ADD TO YOUR ... BROTHERLY KINDNESS, LOVE.

2 PETER 1:5, 7

Kingdom Spotlight
DIFFERENT VIEWS OF THE DOMINION

The kingdom of God was preeminent in the teaching of Jesus. In fact, it was the first thing out of his mouth when he began to preach. "Repent, for the kingdom of heaven is near" (Matt. 3:2).

But for two thousand years we've been trying to figure out how near. Is the kingdom of God here? Is it coming? Is it a little of both?

In the eighteenth century, there was a lot of discussion about the present or future nature of the kingdom of God. Liberal theologians, with their strong emphasis on the social gospel, felt that that the kingdom of God was entirely *now*. The higher-criticism scholars like Dodd and Harnack believed that all that should matter to the church, as far as the kingdom of God was concerned, was how we were going to build it in the here and now. Any references that Jesus made to the kingdom being "future" were either allegorized away or simply dismissed as a later addition by an enthusiastic scribe.

Out of this line of thought came an eschatology known as postmillennialism. Basically, it postulated that since the kingdom of God was being realized on earth, the world would get better and better, and the world would become progressively more Christian so that when Christ returned all he'd have to do is tie up a few loose ends, and we'd have the theocratic utopia described in the latter chapters of the book of Revelation.

Then the First and Second World Wars hit, and people stopped believing that the world was getting better and better. As the likes of Hitler, Stalin, Lenin, Mao Tse-tung, and Mussolini came to power, the church began to look more heavenward for the fulfillment of the kingdom of God. And there became a greater emphasis on the future references to the kingdom of God. The kingdom of God certainly could not be manifesting itself in the midst of such incredible human destruction, so we must look to the heavens for its fulfillment.

Reasonable Christians differ widely on what the kingdom of God will look like after Christ's return. While there's not very many of them left, the postmillennialists believe that the world will get progressively better, increasingly moral, and significantly more Christian. When Christ returns, he will personally carry on the rule and reign prepared for him.

Millennialists tend to be a little more pessimistic about the world's getting better and better. In fact, as the gospel is preached throughout the world, people will become increasingly polarized in their religious views. And with that polarization, increasing animosity will develop.

If you're a dispensational premillennialist, you believe that the church will be raptured, and those left behind will suffer through seven years of tribulation until Christ returns and the millennium begins.

If you're a historic premillennialist (which is where I land), you believe that Christ will return suddenly and unexpectedly to begin the millennium.

Amilliennialists don't believe in a literal thousand-year reign of Christ. They believe that he will simply return and begin the completely fulfilled kingdom of God.

Regardless of your eschatology, the postreturn kingdom of God pretty much looks the same. While the order of service may differ, the end result is almost identical.

And what will that eternal kingdom look like?

While so much of it remains a mystery, we receive clues throughout the Scriptures that give us an idea of what it will be like. As we've talked about, there will be different types, levels, and degrees of responsibility in the postreturn kingdom of God. Second, our heavenly reward is best described by the type, level, and degree of responsibility that we have in that kingdom. The reward/responsibility is based on a relational quality that some might describe as a depth of love, a depth of intimacy, or the ability to clearly give and respond to communication.

For the sake of our purposes here, the relational quality that determines our level of reward and responsibility will be trust—not how much you trust God, but how much he trusts you.

Chapter 12

Love:
The Centurion's Parallel

LOVE: 1. A DEEP, TENDER, INEFFABLE FEELING OF AFFECTION AND SOLICITUDE TOWARD A PERSON. 2. AN INTENSE EMOTIONAL ATTACHMENT. 3. A PERSON WHO IS THE OBJECT OF DEEP OR INTENSE AFFECTION; BELOVED.

DICTIONARY.COM

LOVE IS PATIENT, LOVE IS KIND. IT DOES NOT ENVY, IT DOES NOT BOAST, IT IS NOT PROUD. IT IS NOT RUDE, IT IS NOT SELF-SEEKING, IT IS NOT EASILY ANGERED, IT KEEPS NO RECORD OF WRONGS. LOVE DOES NOT DELIGHT IN EVIL BUT REJOICES WITH THE TRUTH. IT ALWAYS PROTECTS, ALWAYS TRUSTS, ALWAYS HOPES, ALWAYS PERSEVERES. LOVE NEVER FAILS.... AND NOW THESE THREE REMAIN: FAITH, HOPE AND LOVE. BUT THE GREATEST OF THESE IS LOVE.
1 CORINTHIANS 13:4–8, 13

*L*ove is voluntary.

Try reading 1 Corinthians 13 with that modifier, as if it were merely commentary, not, of course, as an "improvement" on the biblical text. "Love is [voluntarily] patient, love is [voluntarily] kind.... If I give all I possess to the poor and surrender my body to the flames, but [do not love voluntarily], I gain nothing" (vv. 4, 3).

The words "I don't really love that person" are hard to say, but Paul seems to imply in 1 Corinthians 13 that those words can accurately describe someone who may be doing all kinds of wonderful things and may think he's showing love, when, in fact, all he's doing is showing off.

KINGDOM SPOTLIGHT

MY VIEW OF THE DOMINION

My eschatology is best described as "historic premillennialism." Bottom line, what that really means is that the dispensationalists (like Tim LaHaye and Jerry Jenkins) won't claim me because I don't believe in a pretribulational rapture. The Reformed theologians, like R. C. Sproul and D. James Kennedy, won't claim me either, because I believe in a literal thousand-year reign of Christ.

Of course, we must never compromise on the essentials of the faith, namely, the indisputable authority of the Scriptures, the deity of Christ, and the presence of at least one guitar during the worship service (just kidding!). However, in my opinion, eschatology is certainly one of the nonessentials of the faith in that our salvation does not depend on what we believe in this area. Whether you're a pre-, post-, or amillennialist, the Lord's going to take you (as a believer) whenever he comes. While your view of what's going to happen in the last days significantly shapes the way you view the church's role in the world, it does not have a bearing on the salvation of your soul.

The judgment of Christians, in my view, will happen shortly after the return of Christ, which will begin the millennium. During this time, Christians will reign with Christ, and the levels of responsibility they are given will depend on the outcome of the test described in this book.

These are the people who love because they "have to" or they're "supposed to." Those who "love" out a sense of compulsion, obligation, or duty but not as a choice for which they are willing to be held morally responsible are just making a lot of noise (like the resounding gongs or clanging cymbals that Paul describes in 1 Corinthians 13:1).

VOLUNTARY LOVE

You can always count on those who love voluntarily. These are the ones who will always protect your relationship, perpetuate hope, persevere during the bad times, and usually give you the benefit of the doubt.

Those who love you voluntarily won't let you get away with garbage either. The saying "Love does not delight in evil but rejoices with the truth" (1 Cor. 13:6) means that sometimes they will practice tough love with you, when caring confrontation increases and vulnerability decreases.

In the same way, God's love for us is voluntary. Loving us is something he's chosen to do, and it's a decision that he's going to stick with. He's not going to coerce, compel, cajole, or humiliate anyone into having a relationship with him. There may be a variety of circumstances that drive us to God, but what keeps us there (by God's grace) is an act of the will for which we're willing to be held accountable.

This is the type of love that Peter wants us to practice and grow in.

It didn't happen too often, but there were times when Jesus seemed genuinely surprised, even stunned and amazed at what he had just encountered. A couple of times it was negative, like when only one out of ten lepers whom he had just healed came back to say thank you (see Luke 17:11–19) or at the lack of faith of the people in his hometown.

On one occasion, he was pleasantly surprised. It was when he encountered the centurion whose servant was sick:

> [In Capernaum] a centurion's servant, whom his master valued highly, was sick and about to die. The centurion heard of Jesus and sent some elders of the Jews to him, asking him to come and heal his servant. When they came to Jesus, they pleaded earnestly with him, "This man deserves to have you do this, because he loves our nation and has built our synagogue." So Jesus went with them.
>
> He was not far from the house when the centurion sent friends to say to him: "Lord, don't trouble yourself, for I do not deserve to have you come under my roof. That is why I did not even consider myself worthy to come to you. But say the word, and my servant will be healed. For I myself am a man under authority, with soldiers under me. I tell this one,

'Go,' and he goes; and that one, 'Come,' and he comes. I say to my servant, 'Do this,' and he does it."

When Jesus heard this, *he was amazed at him,* and turning to the crowd following him, he said, "I tell you, I have not found such great faith even in Israel." Then the men who had been sent returned to the house and found the servant well. (Luke 7:2–10)

What was it about this man's faith that astonished Jesus?

The men who told Jesus about the centurion (a Gentile) said that he loved the people of God. It's interesting to note that in the opinion of these people the centurion *deserved* to have his servant healed because of all he had done for the nation of Israel. But when the humble centurion spoke for himself, he did not claim to deserve anything.

It seems that Jesus was pleased that the man took something he was familiar with (being a man in authority) and *legitimately* drew a parallel between that positive experience and how God probably works. The centurion understood that when he gave an order it would be implemented. The centurion obviously loved the people to whom he gave orders, because he was taking extraordinary measures to get help for one of them when he could not provide it himself.

> *The beginning of love is to let those we love be perfectly themselves, and not to twist them to fit our own image. Otherwise we love only the reflection of ourselves we find in them.*
>
> —THOMAS MERTON

So when Jesus offered to come to the officer's house, the humble man said that that would not be necessary. Because he was a man in authority, he knew how authority worked. And Jesus obviously had supernatural authority, so he should have to do nothing more than say the word and that servant would be healed.

From what we can see in the text, Jesus seemed absolutely delighted with man's attitude (read: "faith").

How can we bring Jesus this type of joy? By drawing *legitimate* parallels between our experience and concluding that God probably works in the same way, especially when it comes to love.

LOVE DEFINED

Of course, that word *legitimate* is significant. Obviously this concept can and has been abused, most tragically perhaps, by injured people who have been raised by abusive or negligent parents and thus conclude that God is either full of rage or completely indifferent to them and what concerns them.

Obviously that picture of God contradicts the Scriptures, regardless of what a person's parents were like, so such a parallel is illegitimate. Any parallel between our experience and how God works cannot contradict what is clearly known about God.

I draw one of these parallels when it comes to my vocation. I suppose that my job can be best described as that of one who "manages creative people." (I work for a publisher and supervise a product development team.) When I tell people what I do in those terms, the response is often humorous. "Manage creative people? Can't be done!" "Just don't hire them in the first place!" "That's like trying to heard a bunch of kittens—don't even try."

But I believe that I'm succeeding because I've had good mentors who have set excellent examples for me. When I was first offered a management position, the man who placed me there gave me this warning: "If I even get a hint that you're micromanaging these talented people, I'll give you so much work that you won't have time to meddle with what they're doing." I took his warning seriously, followed his example, and believe that I'm doing a good job taking his advice.

I've found that the key to successfully managing creative people is to clearly define the objectives and then get out of the way. Of course, it's also a part of my job to check periodically to make sure that the objectives are being reached. But the really hard part is staying out of way and simply letting people be creative.

And the parallel I draw is this: My job as a manager of creative types is to clearly define objectives, make sure that all the people have the resources they need, and let them loose. And the payoff comes when they almost always exceed my expectations and come up with something so good that it would make God smile.

> *We give a lot of freedom to our developers for a reason—they're smart people.*
>
> —BETSY SPEARE,
> RELEASE MANAGER,
> MICROSOFT

And I think that God works in a similar way. He clearly defines the objectives (preach the gospel, help the poor, raise godly children), provides the resources we need (the Word of God, the fellowship of believers, the assurance of his love), and then steps back to see what we'll create with these things.

I think this happened when the Lord visited Abraham. He asked, "Shall I hide from Abraham what I am about to do?" (Gen. 18:17) because God knew that Abraham was going to do something with the information. And he did. He started negotiating. And in good faith, God responded graciously, even though Abraham's final request could not be granted.

God wants to see what we're going to create with what he provides. I don't think we have even begun to grasp how much joy this brings to him. When we come up with something beautiful, something useful, something that honors God, he is delighted. And the last of Peter's traits, the one that seems to encompass them all, is love.

During Jesus' ministry, he seemed supremely concerned that those who identified with him knew how to love one another. And guess how he taught that? He drew legitimate parallels between our experience and God's way of doing things:

> As the Father has loved me, so have I loved you. (John 15:9)

> As I have loved you, so you must love one another. (John 13:34)

> Love your neighbor as yourself. (Matt. 22:39)

In addition to encouraging us to follow Jesus' example, I believe that this last admonition gives us the key to what it means to love people in a practical and meaningful way (to them). The idea of loving others as we love ourselves is also reflected in other biblical teachings:

> So in everything, do to others what you would have them do to you, for this sums up the Law and the Prophets. (Matt. 7:12)

> In this same way, husbands ought to love their wives as their own bodies. He who loves his wife loves himself. (Eph. 5:28)

> Each of you should look not only to your own interests, but also to the interests of others. (Phil. 2:4)

No one likes to be called or thought of as selfish. And love is often defined as *nothing but* self-sacrifice to the needs, wants, and sometimes whims of others. Usually all that produces is a bunch of emotional martyrs who are generally not a lot of fun to be around.

The key to truly loving other people is quite simple: We need to treat their needs, wants, and whims in the same way that we want our own to be treated, to put their interests *on exactly the same plane* as our own, sometimes giving up our preferences for theirs and sometimes doing what's best for ourselves or our families (either way *can* be honoring to God). We need to hold them to the same level of internalized responsibility as we hold ourselves and to love them as we love ourselves.

So when it comes to love,
    it *is* all about you
    and all about the other person
    and all about God
    all at the same time.

Epilogue

According to What You Have Done

The apostle Paul tells in 1 Corinthians 3:13 that God will judge "the quality of each [person's] work" at the judgment seat of Christ.

Peter described various traits that, if they were ours and increasing, would keep us from being ineffective and unproductive in our knowledge of our Lord Jesus Christ and would guarantee a rich welcome into the eternal kingdom.

As we saw in the beginning of this book, the Scriptures tell us repeatedly that God will reward us according to what we have done. Look at the balance between the Old and New Testaments in this. You see exactly the same ideas, with virtually the same wording:

> One thing God has spoken, two things have I heard: that you, O God, are strong, and that you, O Lord, are loving. Surely you will reward each person *according to what he has done.* (Ps. 62:11–12)

> Does not he who weighs the heart perceive it? Does not he who guards your life know it? Will he not repay each person *according to what he has done*? (Prov. 24:12)

> *According to what they have done,* so will he repay wrath to his enemies and retribution to his foes; he will repay the islands their due. (Isa. 59:18)

For the Son of Man is going to come in his Father's glory with his angels, and then he will reward each person *according to what he has done*. (Matt. 16:27)

God "will give to each person *according to what he has done*." (Rom. 2:6)

And I saw the dead, great and small, standing before the throne, and books were opened. Another book was opened, which is the book of life. The dead were judged *according to what they had done* as recorded in the books. The sea gave up the dead that were in it, and death and Hades gave up the dead that were in them, and each person was judged *according to what he had done*. (Rev. 20:12–13)

Behold, I am coming soon! My reward is with me, and I will give to everyone *according to what he has done*. (Rev. 22:12)

One passage that seems to bring all of these ideas together is found in Jeremiah:

I the LORD search the heart and examine the mind, to reward a man according to his conduct, according to what his deeds deserve. (17:10)

First, we are reminded of that dreadfully inconvenient truth that we can hide nothing from God. While others might second-guess our motives (and we theirs), there is not anything in either our hearts or our minds that is not like an open book, with thousands of footnotes and cross-references, that is not at God's disposal instantaneously and without any gaps in his knowledge. God bases his willingness to trust us on this detailed knowledge of us.

Jeremiah reminds us that God rewards according to what he finds in our hearts and minds, according to our conduct, and according to what our deeds deserve. This covers the entirety of the human experience. We are not judged merely on our successes, but according to how we have responded to life in its entirety.

Treasure Hunting

You will be rewarded according to what you did:

>   after you sinned
>   after you failed
>   while you suffered
>   while you recovered
>   while you succeeded
>   while you rested

As we have seen, all of these seasons in life are opportunities to build, lose, or regain God's trust; and they're things that, by God's grace, we can "do" without falling into the trap of thinking that, somehow, we're saved by anything but grace.

Let's look at each one.

Rewarded … After You Sinned

Without a doubt, all sin is a betrayal of God's trust and puts a strain on our relationships with him. However, what happens shortly after the sin can have almost an exponential effect on our relationships with him, causing us to lose or regain his trust.

Consider, once again, the example of the centurion (see Luke 7:2–10). His assumption was that whatever was true for him (relationally) was probably true for God in some way. Remember, this is the type of attitude that amazed Jesus.

Try to think of three or four times when someone blatantly sinned against you and the effect it had on your relationship. If the person dug his or her heels in, remained entrenched in a state of self-justification, and showed no remorse, your ability to trust that person probably took a nosedive. And your relationship was strained.

On the other hand, if a person goes through the ABCM process (which I described earlier)—that is, he Acknowledged that he did something wrong, Bore the burden of the damage to the relationship, did everything humanly possible to Correct the errant behavior, and failing in any of these due to human weakness, wanted to be reconciled with you so much that he asked for Mercy—what would happen to the relationship then? Sure, it may take awhile to rebuild that trust, but in the end, you might end up being even closer to that person.

It's exactly the same way with God.

Our post-sin behavior can pull us closer or drive us further away from God. Of course, some of us may think, *Hey, let's sin so we can get closer to God!* The apostle Paul covered that topic decisively in Romans 7, sufficiently squelching that type to thinking, so don't even think about going down that path.

If you sin, don't deflect responsibility. Confess specifically to the breech you created, and be reconciled with God (and whomever else you sinned against).

The person whom God trusts acknowledges full responsibility when he sins.

Rewarded ... After You Failed

It's common for Christians to associate all failure with sin. Certainly this is true of moral failure. Moral failure and sin are simply synonymous. These are often described as moments of weakness, periods of youthful indiscretion, sudden lapses in common sense, or errors in judgment. But no matter how it's sugarcoated, they are acts of rebellion that alienate God and, usually, people who care about you. When these phrases are used to describe blatant sin, they should be dismissed with the contempt that they deserve.

However, there is a type of failure that really has nothing to do with sin. These failures can be legitimately described as "mistakes."

Perhaps you could take enough logical steps backward and find a sinful reason why you, in the eighth grade, insisted that the cube root of twenty-eight was three; but, really, it was just a mistake.

This is the type of nonsinful failure I'm describing here, and what we do after discovering this type of failure in our lives again provides the opportunity to either build, lose, or regain God's trust. The importance of building God's trust after nonmoral failure is simply this: that you learned from the mistakes you made and that you didn't repeat them (or, if you did, you didn't do so blindly).

The people who do not learn from their mistakes are usually doomed to repeat them. And the reason for this is that they usually attribute the failure to something outside of themselves, something beyond their control. Usually it's other human beings who are somehow connected to the failure. But it could really be anything—circumstances, a bad cold, indigestion, or even the weather. Anything, anything but going through the painful process of internalizing responsibility for the failed direction and then taking corrective action.

But the person who learns from mistakes becomes less and less afraid of making them and, in fact, becomes quite good at failing well. For the person who is actively moving through life, mistakes are going to be made quite frequently. I would much rather be moving in the wrong direction and making midcourse corrections along the way than sitting still in one place too long.

Building or regaining God's trust after failure means picking up the pieces, examining what happened, and trying to prevent the failure from happening again.

Of course, this is the point where we often ask ourselves the guilt-inducing question, "Did I do my best?" When someone defined what "doing my best" actually meant, I was much better able to answer the question.

Doing your best is dependent on three parts: ability, resources, and time. Doing your best often focuses on the first part and ignores the second and third parts.

Imagine a heart surgeon who's the best in the world. She's world renowned for her skill with a scalpel. But put her in a MASH unit with only a pocketknife, under heavy mortar fire, and her "best" is not going to be the same as it might be in a sterile operating room. In this case, her ability has not changed, but the available resources are far different. The surgeries she performs in both environments may have drastically different results, but in both cases she can legitimately claim to have done her best.

Or consider a world-renowned painter of fine-art portraits. He's been practicing his art for thirty years and has every possible color, brush, and utensil at his disposal. But a friend calls him, one to whom he owes a favor, and needs a portrait done for a gallery showing that night. The artist agrees but understands that the final result will not look the same as if he had a couple of weeks to finish the project. In this case, despite his ability and resources, the amount of time he usually has to finish the project is drastically reduced. So his "best" is going to mean something different from what it would be if he had more time.

This is how we build or regain trust with God after nonsinful failure. We have to ask ourselves, "Did I do my best, according to the ability, time, and resources that were available to me?" Again, God knows the exact answer to each of those three factors. If you dropped the ball in any of these areas, it's best to just acknowledge it up front. God knows our hearts better than we do; if we want to enjoy his trust, we simply need to acknowledge what's true.

That's the first step.

Second, after we've made this assessment, we try to see how we could do better the next time. When I bring bad news to my boss, he not only wants to hear a solution, but also wants to know how this particular crisis can be prevented in the future.

Was it a problem with ability? Do you need some sort of training? Were you not able to accomplish something simply because you didn't know how or you didn't know the best way? If so, how do you obtain that ability?

Be careful to look out for illegitimate excuses here, self-sabotaging phrases that say, "Oh, I could never do that because of my [fill in the blank: weight, gender, handicap, race, family of origin, low self-esteem, fear, etc.]." Out of the eight billion people who have existed since the garden of Eden, there was probably at least one who had your particular challenge and found a way to overcome it.

If you're lacking in a particular ability, do whatever is reasonable (not necessarily easy) to increase or even gain that particular skill.

Next, ask what resources were available to you. When you face that situation again, how can you increase the chances that you will have what you need?

And what about time? Were you rushed? Or was there so much time that you didn't feel sufficient pressure until it was too late? Again, how can you prevent this from being a problem in the future?

Ability. Time. Resources. These are the criteria by which we measure our "best" efforts in any particular situation and how we can build or regain God's trust after we fail.

The person whom God trusts fails well and frequently, is not afraid to examine what went wrong, and has the courage and motivation to make needed corrections along the way.

Rewarded ... While You Suffered

As we talked about earlier, we live in the best of all possible worlds, one in which exists free will, that condition that holds all people morally responsible for their thoughts, words, and actions. And sometimes others' decisions result in significant loss and intense suffering in our lives.

As a result of our suffering, we can pursue one of two paths: We can become either bitter or better. The path we choose will affect God's willingness to trust us.

All bets are off when we are in the middle of suffering. Complaints, grief, confusion, loudly expressed frustration—they are all allowed, permission granted. While God is going to take what you say very seriously, he's not going to hold it against you if it's simply a temporary expression of your pain. Or perhaps we should say that he will understand that these are the thoughts and words of a person in deep agony and accept them accordingly.

However, the opportunity to build or lose God's trust usually comes after the trial. When the pain is passed, how have we been changed? Have we become bitter or better?

Bitterness is best defined as an acidic and preventable response to trauma or suffering of any kind. In rare cases, bitterness can form a transitory, protective hedge around someone who is in an abusive situation. But the goal is to make the hedge temporary and remove it when the source of the danger has been removed.

However, for some, bitterness becomes a refuge and a reason to project painful feelings on to other people. The source of the original danger has passed, and yet they hold on to their hatred and resentment—because they have become familiar friends.

Becoming "better" after we've suffered may mean we have a greater appreciation for God's peace, something that perhaps we once took for granted. "Better" could mean a greater ability to empathize with the pain of others. In these cases, "we can comfort those in any trouble with the comfort we ourselves have received from God" (2 Cor. 1:4). "Better" may mean a newly discovered ability to empathize with God's suffering, which in itself can be one of the most intimate forms of worship that a human being can experience.

Our response to suffering may create in us the ability to go beyond feeling sorry for someone (which is sympathy) to actually being able to experience, or relate deeply to, the feelings of someone who is going through a traumatic time. Quite often this will begin the healing process for someone who is deeply troubled.

The person whom God trusts does not remain bitter when the trial of suffering has passed but instead becomes "better," better able to empathize with the suffering of God and others.

Rewarded ... While You Recovered

> They came to Bethsaida, and some people brought a blind man and begged Jesus to touch him. He took the blind man by the hand and led him outside the village. When he had spit on the man's eyes and put his hands on him, Jesus asked, "Do you see anything?"
>
> He looked up and said, "I see people; they look like trees walking around."
>
> Once more Jesus put his hands on the man's eyes. Then his eyes were opened, his sight was restored, and he saw everything clearly. (Mark 8:22–25)

Why did it take two tries here? Some have suggested that the man might have been blind from birth so he did not have the ability to psychologically interpret the new things that he was seeing. On the second "healing" he was able to interpret what he saw.

Two healings: one physical, one psychological.

I'm guessing they're all like that.

The process of recovery after suffering (assuming we are the following the "better" way) is also a season in which we can build or regain God's trust. And again, there are two paths we can take: permanent retreat or cautious progress.

One of the greatest stories of recovery is that of Elijah's flight to the wilderness. God had just demonstrated his magnificent power against the prophets of Baal, but now Jezebel, the Baal matriarch, was after Elijah. In his distress, Elijah simply begged God to take his life because he had no hope for escape from the relentless evil of Jezebel.

In response, God told Elijah to have something to eat and take a nap. After he had time to rest, he was able to get back in the game and keep participating in incredible demonstrations of God's power.

The keys to Elijah's recovery were these:

1. The time of retreat was absolutely necessary.
2. It was temporary.

We must not cling to the fabled notion that we must never quit, never stop relenting in our goal. Sometimes quitting, at least for a short period of time, is necessary in order for us to fully recover and, once we have regained our bearing, to go on and do additional great things for God. James reminds us that Elijah "was a man just like us" (5:17), so what worked for him will work for us.

But then there are those who retreat permanently, never to trust again, never to become appropriately vulnerable again. There needs to be room for much grace here, especially when the trauma has been so egregious that no one, humanly speaking, can even move toward vulnerability. God knows what that person is capable of, and if rendered incapable, then certainly there are enough time and grace to find the appropriate help.

But those who insist that they're just fine, that they have no need to rest, try to do so as a demonstration of strength that may or may not actually be there. If it's not there, and there has not been sufficient time for them to recover, the result is often sudden and abrupt burnout.

The amount of recovery time that is needed varies depending on the person and the seriousness of the trauma. What's important, no matter what, is that the time of retreat is taken and that it's temporary.

The person whom God trusts takes time to recover after a serious loss and, when sufficiently rested, gets back on the horse that threw him off.

Rewarded ... While You Succeeded

This is the area that most people think about when it comes to being judged for our works—not that we simply did acts of service, but that we were successful, that we bore fruit.

And the hard truth is that, yes, this does matter to God. As it matters to stockholders that their investments bear a return, as it's important to teachers that students grasp certain concepts, as it's important to managers that those they supervise maintain acceptable levels of productivity, so our fruitfulness matters to God.

This is what's commonly known as "works," really doing something in order to be rewarded by God. God is rightly concerned with our effectiveness, that we're producing more than what we started out with. Making money, as in the stewardship parable, is often a helpful analogy. Sometimes it is more than an analogy; it is the very thing that God wants us to do. In any case, God is supremely concerned with growth, that these traits are ours (that is, that we possess them) and that they are increasing.

While sin, failure, and suffering may thwart our efforts, God does not want or expect this to be the norm for us. What's important is that we're moving forward—except, again, for brief periods of retreat and regrouping. The traits that Peter describes need to be ours, but we also need to experience some sort of maturity.

And where should we be bearing fruit; where should we be succeeding? We must look first to our natural talents and our spiritual gifts. We know which ones we have because when we exercise them they bring us joy and satisfaction.

Granted, there are times when doing our jobs and performing ministry is very mundane and sometimes frustrating, but if we're doing the thing for which God has created us, there's always a sense that we're moving in the right direction. But if joylessness is the norm, then it's time to figure out what's wrong.

WHAT AFFECTS OUR ABILITY TO BEAR FRUIT?

First and foremost, we must abide in Christ.

> I am the true vine, and my Father is the gardener. He cuts off every branch in me that bears no fruit, while every branch that does bear fruit he prunes so that it will be even more fruitful. You are already clean because of the word I have spoken to you. Remain in me, and I will remain in you. No branch can bear fruit by itself; it must remain in the vine. Neither can you bear fruit unless you remain in me. I am the vine; you are the branches. If a man remains in me and I in him, he will bear much fruit; apart from me you can do nothing. If anyone does not remain in me, he is

Of course, we're not going to succeed all the time. But if we're acknowledging our sin, making midcourse corrections when we fail, counting our losses, and grieving properly when we suffer, then we can't help but eventually succeed. This is the norm; if we work the system, then the system will eventually bear fruit.

Again, one of my favorite verses in the Old Testament is this:

> Remember the LORD your God, for it is he who gives you the ability to produce wealth. (Deut. 8:18)

In the context of this passage, the Lord was anticipating that once the Israelites got settled and started accumulating resources, they would one day forget him. Forgetting God diminishes his trust. Remembering him, acknowledging him as the source of our abilities and the giver of the time and resources to use that ability, builds trust.

When it comes to bearing fruit, we must also keep in mind that apart from Jesus we can do nothing. We must abide in him. Abiding in Jesus, according to Michael Breen, simply means to rest in such a way that the Holy Spirit can renew our bodies, minds, and spirits so that we can tackle the new challenges that he has in store for us.[1]

The person whom God trusts consistently bears spiritual fruit with the time, resources, and ability that God has provided.

And that leads us to our final season.

Reward ... While You Rested

God commands us to rest. It's in the Ten Commandments, and we see Jesus doing it all the time during his ministry. If and how we rest can have a significant impact on God's willingness to trust us.

To effectively rest simply means to reenergize.

For those who like to split people into two different groups, there are two different ways to reenergize, namely, one for introverts and one for extroverts. Generally speaking, introverts need time alone to reenergize and then spend that energy around people. Extroverts are energized by being around people and by doing things together with others. Time alone for them tends to be draining.

> like a branch that is thrown away and withers; such branches are picked up, thrown into the fire and burned. (John 15:1–6)

According to Michael Breen, author of *A Passionate Life*, we must move from rest to work, and this is the time to abide in Christ. After we come out of this time of rest, only then are we to enter into our work and start bearing fruit.

According to Breen, since Adam and Eve were created on the sixth day of creation, the first "task" that God assigned to them was to rest (with him) on the seventh day. And then from the rest they were able to go forth into the garden to bear figurative and literal fruit. Therefore the biblical model seems to be that we move from rest to work, rather than from work to rest. Once we have our bearings for the week, abiding in Christ, listening to the Spirit, and refreshing our souls, only then are we ready to venture forth and produce fruit for the kingdom.

Of course, the type of activity, for both the introvert (alone) and the extrovert (with others), has a lot to do with how rested they become. Neither the introvert who puts on a seminar nor the extrovert who goes on a hike by himself will likely be refreshed. Each has to decide for himself or herself what works best.

Resting allows both the body and the mind to relax and reflect, not only on what's happened, but also on what is anticipated. It allows the mind to be quieted so that the Spirit of God can speak to us.

Again, for the introvert this will probably best happen alone, in a bookstore or similar quiet space. For the extrovert, it might happen over a cup of coffee with a friend. Some people think out loud, and it's helpful for them to first express their thoughts so that they can sort them out with a friend.

Avoiding effective rest diminishes God's ability to trust us. First of all, we're avoiding a clear command. Everyone should have a full day off every week, preferably a day devoted to worship. And besides, it's harder to trust a tired person. The one thing that seemed to irritate Jesus in the garden of Gethsemane was his friends' fatigue. They wanted to be with him, but their bodies simply would not cooperate. Without the needed rest, they were unavailable to support Jesus during his hour of crisis. You can bet that when Judas and his armed friends arrived, the disciples were wide awake.

The person whom God trusts knows how to effectively reenergize.

Treasures in Heaven

The treasure that we store in heaven, what we "send on ahead" and what moth and dust do not corrupt, is the depth and breadth of God's willingness to trust us.

All the tangible expressions of that treasure—jewels, crowns, mansions, thrones, power, authority, and responsibility—are a reflection of how much God trusts each of us.

So you must ask yourself these questions:
- Do I understand, and have I experienced, the grace of God?
- Have I entered into the kingdom of God? Does the foundation of saving faith, upon which I can build God's trust, even exist in my heart?
- In what situation(s) do I find myself at this moment: sinning, failing, suffering, recovering, succeeding, or resting?
- How can I use these experiences to recover the trust that I might have lost with God or to build upon the trust that I have already gained with him?

May the Lord find you to be a trustworthy servant—and reward you accordingly.

READERS' GUIDE

FOR PERSONAL REFLECTION OR GROUP DISCUSSION

PREFACE

1. How do you think each of the following people perceives heaven: the billionaire, the Hollywood celebrity, the homeless alcoholic? What do you think heaven will be like?

2. If God chose you instead of Job, in what areas of your life would Satan challenge your integrity?

3. What do you think God is doing to prepare believers for life in heaven?

4. Do you tend to trust people until they do something to violate that trust, or do you wait to put your confidence in them until they've proved themselves trustworthy? Explain your preference.

5. How do you reconcile the fact that God extends grace to us but also holds us accountable for our actions?

CHAPTER 1

1. How does the author define the "Final Dominion"? How does this view fit into your view of what's going to happen in the last days?

2. The Bible confirms that Pilate and Nero were given their authority by God (see John 19:11; Rom. 13:1). Who would you consider a contemporary Pilate or Nero? What do you think God is trying to accomplish through these power abusers?

3. If there are no enemies or conflicts to resolve in heaven, what will motivate you?

4. What are some responsibilities that God has given to Christians that may prepare them well for positions of responsibility in Jesus' kingdom?

5. What have you created that God delights in? What kinds of "things" could you make that would bring God joy?

Chapter 2

1. Does grace make evaluation meaningless? Why or why not?
2. How does the inevitability of the judgment seat of Christ motivate you to serve God?
3. The author teaches that there will be degrees of reward in heaven that will be "types and levels of responsibility in the Final Dominion." What might those types and levels of responsibility be? Will "equality" be a characteristic in heaven if such levels of responsibility exist? Why or why not?
4. What drives you more, the fear of loss or the anticipation of reward? Do you consider one to be more godly or honorable than the other? Why?
5. Of the sixteen desires listed, which ones would be your top three motivations? How could these desires manifest themselves as heavenly rewards and responsibilities?

Chapter 3

1. What precautions should one take when interpreting a Bible passage allegorically?
2. How do you measure the fruitfulness of your actions?
3. What's the closest experience you've had to heaven on earth? What can you learn about heaven from that experience?
4. Why do you agree or disagree that every Christian will be held accountable for his or her sins at the judgment seat of Christ?
5. What's God's ROI (return on investment) from your life: a loss, breakeven, doubled, thirty-, sixty-, or one hundredfold? What would your life look like at each of these percentages?

Chapter 4

1. What incidents of mercy have you seen God extend to the unsaved? How has he shown mercy to you?
2. If you believe yourself to be a former (or current) enemy of God, what would your "most wanted" poster say as it hung in heaven's post office?
3. What's the difference between having a personal relationship with Jesus and having a reconciled relationship with him?
4. Does it seem fair that some Christians take front and center stage because they led notoriously evil lives before being reconciled with God? Explain.
5. Why does God's generosity with others occasionally irk us?

6. Who is the most unlikely person in your life to ever come to Christ? How would the kingdom of God benefit if that person was reconciled with the Lord?

Chapter 5

1. What does belief without repentance look like? What does repentance without belief look like?
2. Do you think anyone goes through life without some kind of faith? Explain.
3. Put these statements in the proper chronological order. Indicate if any of them happen simultaneously.
  I accepted Jesus.
  I accepted Jesus as Savior.
  I accepted Jesus as Lord.
  I accepted Jesus as Savior and Lord.
  Explain.
4. Is genuine repentance an acknowledgment of Christ's lordship? Explain.

Chapter 6

1. What kind of peer pressure did you experience as a kid? What kinds of peer pressure do you experience now as an adult?
2. How would an intelligent, compassionate non-Christian describe you?
3. Do you consider yourself an exodus or an exile Christian? In your opinion, is it more effective to transform culture from within or from the outside looking in?
4. Where are you on the contentment-growth continuum? Explain.
5. Where do you draw the line when it comes to interacting with a culture that is hostile to the claims of Christ?

Chapter 7

1. If you could ask God any question, what would it be? Where might you find the answer to that question this side of heaven?
2. True or false: Every problem has a solution. Explain.
3. What set of clothes do you own now that might represent acceptable attire at the heavenly wedding banquet? Explain your analogy.
4. How is the truth trampled on these days? Is withholding the truth, regardless of the circumstances, the same thing as lying?

5. When have you been motivated by fear? By love? Which was more effective in their respective situations? Explain.

Chapter 8

1. If your life were a corporation, how much of the stock would you own? If there are other people who own stock in the company of your life, what percentage of shares do they own?

2. What characteristic of God do you most clearly reflect? Where is that reflection the dullest?

3. All of our actions have consequences. When we do something that's unwise, sometimes the consequences are far more severe than we think is fair. If that happened to you, how would that impact your ability to internalize responsibility for the original stupid action?

4. In your opinion, what are the essentials of the faith? In what nonessential of the faith is God expecting consistency and authenticity from you?

5. How is your kingdom doing today?

Chapter 9

1. How did you emotionally respond to the statement "We live in the best of all possible worlds"? Why did you have that reaction?

2. List ten of the most significant losses in your life. Has any of these affected your perception of how much, or how little, God loves you?

3. Of all the biblical characters who experienced significant loss in their lives, with which one do you most closely identify? Explain.

4. What better describes your expectations for life: a five-star hotel or a concentration camp? If neither, what in-between metaphor might you choose?

5. In what area of your life would you be most willing to give up free will if you could be absolved from the responsibility of your actions? Explain.

Chapter 10

1. How do you distinguish between really hearing the voice of God and just talking to yourself?

2. If you felt that God was speaking to you or leading you to do a particular thing, who would you ask for confirmation? What "test" would that person apply?

3. What was humble about the way that the woman at the well told her neighbors about Christ?

4. How sensitive is your spiritual radar? How can you tell when the Holy Spirit has been working in a person's life or in your own?

5. Draw a target with several concentric circles. What would the circles represent in terms of your areas of ministry and influence?

CHAPTER 11

1. With what type of person do you most easily empathize?

2. Did you ever have a painful experience in your life that was caused by the maliciousness of another? As a result of this experience, where would you place yourself on the bitter-to-better scale?

3. How can personal pain better enable a believer to empathize with God's suffering?

4. Why is evil often described as the absence of empathy?

5. On a scale of one to ten, how much do you think God trusts you? What would need to happen for that rating to go up one point?

CHAPTER 12

1. What does involuntary love look like?

2. What are some meaningful synonyms for *love* for you? For example, what word would you substitute for *love* in 1 Corinthians 13?

3. What legitimate parallels can you draw from your own station or role in life to better understand how God relates to people?

4. Complete the following label:
   Loving only myself: selfishness
   Loving only others: relational martyrdom
   Loving myself and others, placing the interests of others on the same plane as my own, occasionally sacrificing, occasionally receiving: _____

EPILOGUE

1. Identify the people in your life who exemplify each of Peter's traits:
   Faith: _____
   Goodness: _____
   Knowledge: _____
   Self-Control: _____
   Perseverance: _____
   Godliness: _____

You Can Take It with You!

Kindness: _____

Love: _____

How would you like to be more like those people? What can you take from their example and incorporate into your life?

2. Describe a nonsinful failure in your life. Did you repeat it? What did you learn from it?

3. Do you reenergize better when you're alone or when you're around certain people?

4. What does God see clearly that you typically hide from others?

5. Which material will predominantly characterize your experience at the judgment seat of Christ—"gold, silver, precious stones, wood, hay, [or] stubble" (1 Cor. 3:12 KJV)?

Bibliography

Alcorn, Randy. *Heaven*. Wheaton, IL: Tyndale House, 2004.

Breen, Michael, and Walt Kallestad. *A Passionate Life*. Colorado Springs: Cook Communications, 2005.

Camus, Albert. *The Plague*. Translated by Stuart Gilbert. New York: Vintage, 1991.

CNN.com. "Ex-hostage: 'I wanted to gain his trust.'" CNN.com, March 14, 2005. http://www.cnn.com/2005/LAW/03/14/smith.transcript/.

Detweiler, Craig, and Barry Taylor. *A Matrix of Meanings: Finding God in Pop Culture*. Grand Rapids: Baker, 2003.

Haralson, Hal. *Gentle Mercies: Stories of Faith in Faded Blue Jeans*. Colorado Springs: Cook Communications, 2001.

Hendra, Tony. *Father Joe: The Man Who Saved My Soul*. New York: Random House, 2004.

Lewis, C. S. *That Hideous Strength*. New York: Scribner, 2003.

———. *Letters to Malcolm: Chiefly on Prayer*. Eugene, OR: Harvest Books, 2002.

Luce, Ron. *Battle Cry for a Generation*. Colorado Springs: Cook Communications, 2005.

Machiavelli, Niccolo. *The Prince*. Translated by Daniel Donno. New York: Bantam, 1984.

Reiss, Steven. *Who Am I? The 16 Basic Desires That Motivate Our Actions and Define Our Personalities*. New York: Berkley Books, 2002.

Ryken, Leland. *How to Read the Bible as Literature*. Grand Rapids: Zondervan, 1985.

Schmidt, Doug. *The Prayer of Revenge: Forgiveness in the Face of Injustice*. Colorado Springs: Cook Communications, 2003.

Smith, Ashley, and Stacy Mattingly. *Unlikely Angel: The Untold Story of the Atlanta Hostage Hero*. Grand Rapids: Zondervan, 2005.

Tzu, Sun. *The Art of War*. Philadelphia: Running Press, 2003.

Wikipedia, s.v. "Twelve-Step Program," http://en.wikipedia.org/wiki/12-step.

Willard, Dallas. *The Divine Conspiracy: Rediscovering Our Hidden Life in God*. San Francisco: HarperSanFrancisco, 1998.

NOTES

PREFACE

1. Mitch Albom, *The Five People You Meet in Heaven* (New York: Hyperion, 2003).
2. Howard A. Johnson, http://cqod.gospelcom.net/cqodndag.htm.
3. Ashley Smith and Stacy Mattingly, *Unlikely Angel: The Untold Story of the Atlanta Hostage Hero* (Grand Rapids: Zondervan, 2005).
4. CNN.com. "Ex-hostage: 'I wanted to gain his trust,'" March 14, 2005, http://www.cnn.com/2005/LAW/03/14/smith.transcript/.

CHAPTER 1

1. Randy Alcorn, *Heaven* (Wheaton, IL: Tyndale House, 2004).

CHAPTER 2

1. C. S. Lewis, *Letters to Malcolm: Chiefly on Prayer* (Eugene, OR: Harvest Books, 2002).
2. Ibid.
3. G. K. Chesterton, http://aquinasrcia.blogspot.com/2004/11/week-5-and-6-original-sin-and-theodicy.html.
4. Steven Reiss, *Who Am I? The 16 Basic Desires That Motivate Our Actions and Define Our Personalities* (New York: Berkley Books, 2002).

CHAPTER 3

1. Albert Schweitzer, *The Quest of the Historical Jesus* (London: A & C Black, 1936).
2. Eustathius, "De Engastrimytho contra Origenem," in *Texte und Untersuchungen zur Geschichte der altchristlichen Literatur,* trans. A. Jahn (New York: Walter de Gruyter & Co., 1992).
3. Dallas Willard, *The Divine Conspiracy: Rediscovering Our Hidden Life in God* (San Francisco: HarperSanFrancisco, 1998).

CHAPTER 4

1. John Tillotson, http://www.worldofquotes.com/topic/christianity/20.
2. C. S. Lewis, *Surprised by Joy* (New York: Harcourt, 1955).

CHAPTER 5

1. Leland Ryken, *How to Read the Bible as Literature* (Grand Rapids: Zondervan, 1985).
2. David C. Downing, *The Most Reluctant Convert: C. S. Lewis's Journey to Faith* (Downers Grove, IL: InterVarsity Press, 2002).
3. "Antony Flew Abandons Atheism," http://www.existence-of-god.com/flew-abandons-atheism.html.
4. Democritus, http://www.heartquotes.net/happiness.html.
5. *Wall Street*, Directed by Oliver Stone, Hollywood, CA: 20th Century Fox, 1987.

CHAPTER 6

1. "Condoleezza Rice," *Power for Living*, March 6, 2005.
2. Mohandas Gandhi, http://www.brainyquote.com/quotes/quotes/m/mohandasga160735.html.
3. Niccolo Machiavelli, *The Prince*, trans. Daniel Donno (New York: Bantam Classics, 1984).

CHAPTER 7

1. Nick Butterworth and Mick Inkpen, *Wonderful Earth!* (Elgin, IL: Chariot Books, 1990).
2. *Encyclopaedia Britannica*, http://corporate.britannica.com/press/inventions.html.
3. Paul Lundquist, "Thought for the Week," February 26, 2004, http://www.forministry.com/USILEFREEFBCFB/messagefromourpastor.dsp.

CHAPTER 8

1. Wikipedia, "Twelve-Step Program," http://en.wikipedia.org/wiki/12-step.
2. *Merriam-Webster's Dictionary*, 15th ed., s.v. "locus."
3. Willard, *Divine Conspiracy*.
4. Ibid.
5. Ibid.

CHAPTER 9

1. Gottfried Wilhelm Leibniz, *Discourse on Metaphysics and the Monadology*, trans. R. Montgomery (Amherst, NY: Prometheus, 1992).
2. C. S. Lewis, *Mere Christianity* (San Francisco: HarperSanFrancisco, 2001).
3. Leslie Weatherhead, *The Will of God* (Nashville: Abingdon Press, 1999).
4. C. S. Lewis, "Answers to Questions on Christianity," in *God in the Dock* (Grand Rapids: Eerdmans, 1970).

5. C. S. Lewis, *A Grief Observed* (San Francisco: HarperSanFrancisco, 1961).
6. Ron Luce, *Battle Cry for a Generation* (Colorado Springs: Cook Communications, 2005).

CHAPTER 10

1. Mirabel Osler, *In the Eye of the Garden* (New York: Macmillan, 1994).
2. Willard, *Divine Conspiracy.*

CHAPTER 11

1. Hal Haralson, *Gentle Mercies: Stories of Faith in Faded Blue Jeans.* (Colorado Springs: Cook Communications, 2001).

EPILOGUE

1. Michael Breen and Walt Kallestad, *A Passionate Life* (Colorado Springs: Cook Communications, 2005).